M000303863

The
Blue Garter
Club

The
Blue Garter
Club

Ties That Bind
Fourteen ChristianWomen
for Forty Years

Carol Wade Lee

LANGMARC PUBLISHING • **San Antonio, Texas**

The Blue Garter Club

Ties That Bind Fourteen
Christian Women for Forty Years

By Carol Wade Lee

Editor: Renée Hermanson

Cover by Michael Qualben

Text Illustrations by Susan Q. Reue

Copyright © 1992 by Carol Wade Lee
First Printing 1992, Second Printing 1993
Printed in the United States of America
All rights reserved. Written permission
must be secured from the publisher to
reproduce any part of this book.

Published by LangMarc Publishing
Box 33817, San Antonio, TX 78265

Library of Congress Cataloging-in-Publication Data

Lee, Carol Wade
    The Blue Garter Club: ties that bind fourteen Christian women for forty
years / Carol Wade Lee
    p. cm.
ISBN 1-880292-20-3
1. Concordia College (Moorhead, Minn.) —Alumni—Biography. 2. Women
college graduates—United States—Biography. 3. Women college graduates—United States—Religious life. I. Title.
LD1281. C30671L44   1992   CIP
378. 776'91—dc20   92-4563

In Memory of

Stephanie

Contents

Thank You

To all of the members of
The Blue Garter Club,
who willingly shared their stories.

Thanks to my husband for his
patience, insight and encouragement.
Thank you to Lois for her constant encouragement
and assistance; for poetry contributions from
Daphne Lewis (Illuminations: An Interweave of
Thought, Identity, and Love); Dee Hoff Larson,
Lois Qualben; lyrics of John Ylvisaker;
to Susan Q. Reue for her text illustrations,
Joyce Sonnabend for her "Farewell" art,
Michael Qualben for his cover design and photography.

Foreword

The Blue Garter Club is not a book about ordinary people. It might appear that these fourteen women were ordinary in the sense that they were products of Middle America in the 1950s. They were the Depression born children of stable families in which the parents worked hard, sacrificed for their children, were the backbone of their mainline congregations and set high moral standards. As products of their time and culture, these fourteen planned to work hard, worship faithfully and fulfill traditional roles as wives and mothers.

But as they graduated from college and formed their Blue Garter Club in 1956, there was no way they could have anticipated the extraordinary cultural and social changes which they would experience in the next 36 years. They would be a transition generation as they combined career and family in different ways and for longer periods of time than most had expected. They would experience economic setbacks and generation gaps, dependencies and death, betrayal and estrangement, unemployment and job discrimination. Along with all of that, they would be more open to feelings and more expressive in their relationships than was true of preceding generations.

As these stories unfold it becomes clear that these fourteen are extraordinary people. Their marriages remained stable in a generation when divorce rates soared, they engaged in meaningful vocation through a variety of careers, they provided leadership in stable and high achieving families and they rendered distinguished service in their churches and communities. While they would live their lives in a culture very different from the one they had experienced and expected, they would do so with distinction, character and faithfulness.

And how do we explain the extraordinary lives of these people born into ordinary circumstances? There is a lot to be learned here about the care and tending of strong marriages, the importance of grace and perseverance in parenting, the role of unifying traditions, the importance of good education and life long learning, and the place of attitudes which blend flexibility and stability. But the most striking lesson of these stories is the rock-like place of Christian faith in shaping and sustaining life. That theme is reiterated time and again in those key events in which the Word became flesh in the lives of these women.

These fourteen women were my college classmates and are now loyal alumni of the college which I now lead. It was the college that brought them together forty years ago, and it is the college's motto, Soli Deo Gloria— to God Alone the Glory—which binds them together still. They are "world changers" and their stories of grace and service are parables worth telling.

Paul Dovre, Ph.D.
President, Concordia College

Introduction

"A good acquaintance is a jewel,
a special friend is a treasure."

The mail has arrived. I recognize the fat manila envelope covered with stamps—the Round Robin. Each time it arrives, warm waves of anticipation envelop me as I retrieve it from the mailbox, pour myself a cup of coffee, and settle into my easy chair for a couple of hours of sheer joy. This Robin has been flying steadily for 36 years—carrying a collection of letters written by a group of women who became friends at Concordia College, Moorhead, Minnesota, in the early 1950s.

Reading the Robin takes some time because there are 14 letters, as well as pictures, to be savored. Special attention gets paid to weight, gray hair, and possible wrinkles. When I finish the last letter, I stare at the verse on my coffee mug: *"A good acquaintance is a jewel, a special friend is a treasure."* Thoughts of these special friends, these treasures, fill my head. I reminisce about this Round Robin group, our days at Concordia, where we roomed together, attended classes together, and played together. And where we started The Blue Garter Club.

Wearing the same blue garter when each of us was married became a pact that held us together. This blue garter made the wedding rounds to become our symbol of belonging to a group whose friendships we treasured, individually and collectively. Within a few years, that blue garter had outlived its symbolic usefulness and was finally packed away by the last member to pledge her marriage vows. Yet the friendship pact didn't end with the last wearing of the garter. The Blue Garter

Club members became our Round Robin participants, still bonded through 36 years.

My thoughts turn to these individuals and what has transpired in each member's life over the past 36 years. Collectively, this group of women has experienced almost everything that any woman might contemplate happening to her in her own lifetime—joys and sorrows, achievements and setbacks. Through everything, the club's members have grown in Christ and have known God's sustaining presence in their lives.

At Concordia's 1991 Homecoming, our group planned a luncheon for our 35th class reunion. I proposed having a newspaper article written about the group that had stayed in such close contact for so many years. But instead, a publisher friend suggested a book be written about these women. So at our reunion luncheon, I asked the Blue Garter Club members if they would participate by sharing their experiences. Some were reluctant; some were cynical. But everyone was willing to share. One thing they did agree upon was that names would have to be changed to protect the innocent!

During the months that followed, I considered how our sometimes-ordinary lives have taken some anguished twists and cruel turns. When we embarked on our new lives after graduation, we thought mostly of the happiness ahead: careers, marriage, children. The '50s image of marital bliss was a little vine-covered cottage surrounded by a white picket fence with happy, immaculate children playing in the yard. But, descriptions of our first homes bear no resemblance whatsoever to that vine-covered cottage!

Our dreams for the future centered around teaching careers and long marriages. Missing from those dreams were the realities of other events that barged into our lives: adoption, widowhood, loss of a child, birth of a mentally-handicapped child, alcoholism, bankruptcy, military life, cancer, a homosexual husband, advanced degrees, employment changes, political office, sexual harassment, owning a business.

Life styles within the group have varied just as much—from the traditional (wife and mother stays at home), to the more typical (wife and mother works outside the home), to the unique (the wife and children often living a life separate from their husband-father, enjoying periodic reunions for the whole family).

...And now there are fourteen

In college there were 15 of us in The Blue Garter Club. Now there are 14. Marion was killed in a car accident twenty years ago. A drunk driver speeding through a red light hit her car broadside, pushing it into oncoming traffic, causing a pile-up of several vehicles. Marion died instantly and several others were injured. Losing a member of our close-knit group in such a tragic way saddened all of us. It also brought us closer together; we treasured our friendships even more.

I thought of petite, vivacious Marion, with her brown wavy hair; she always looked younger than her age. That was irritating to her during her college years. I remember how she washed her hair, combed and pushed the waves into place, and then sat reading a book for a half hour while it dried. We envied her. She married her high school sweetheart from Minneapolis.

...And then came Alli

A small-world experience popped up when Marion's 26-year-old daughter, Allis Anne, attended a gathering in my neighborhood. 'Alli Reed' was written on her name tag. Because she looked so much like Marion, I inquired about a possible relationship. Alli was surprised to learn that I was her mother's friend in college, and that I even had baby pictures of Alli in my photo album. Getting to know Alli was easy. She's talkative, like her mother. We got together for lunch, dinner, and evening chats. Age didn't seem to be a barrier.

Alli confided that she'd been depressed lately because her job involved working with people who were about to be laid off. She'd earned a master's degree in psychology, then accepted a position as a personnel counselor for a large manufacturing company in our city. Layoffs were imminent. Her heart ached for people who faced unemployment. She said she was considering going back to school to earn a Ph.D. in psychology.

Alli yearned to know more about her mother, who died when Alli was only six. Even though her grandmother had talked a lot about Marion, so many unanswered questions remained. Who was her mother? What was her life like when she was in college? Who were her friends in college? What did she think? What was important to her? What would she do now if she were in Alli's shoes?

As I listened to Alli talk about her concerns and feelings, I wondered how her mother's death had been dealt with by her family twenty years ago. She seemed to be focusing an unhealthy interest in her dead mother at a very transitional period in her own life. Had she been allowed to adequately grieve her mother's untimely death? Twenty years ago, was the family so involved in their own grief, they failed to realize that a six-year-old child needed to grieve, too?

It struck me as ironic: Twenty years ago Alli lost her mother, who was my age. Twenty years ago I lost a daughter, close to Alli's age. Would we become surrogate mother/daughter?

Alli asked me questions about what college life was like for us. When I told her about the book we were writing, her interest increased. Since we'd planned a Blue Garter Club reunion for the purpose of working on the book, I asked if she'd like to attend our gathering and get acquainted with the other women who were her mother's best friends in college. She jumped at the chance, even offering to operate the tape recorder. When she said she had a million questions to ask everyone, the thought occurred to me that she'd be a good moderator. It would be refreshing and stimulating to have a next-generation woman set the tone of our reunion.

Alli's reaction to my invitation was to treat it like a major assignment for a psychology class. She went to the attic and searched through her mother's old cedar chest. Along with wedding memorabilia, she found the 1956 Concordia yearbook. Using my address list, she located each Blue Garter Club member, cut out and pasted each senior picture on a separate poster. Next she researched each member's school activities, including her mother's, thus learning something about each person. Alli inquired about each one's family, vocation and location, adding this pertinent information to the bottom of each page. She sent each member a set of questions to answer. After preliminary conversations with several participants, I outlined the book's format for Alli, and she gained a sense of the variations among the life styles of the women involved.

Knowing that time was limited during the weekend reunion, we identified Alli's main tasks as moderator. (1) She will keep the dialogue moving on track to discourage rambling; (2) She will read from the narrative I prepared in advance to ensure that a history and a foundation are in place for facilitating discussion; (3) She will motivate members to tell their stories; (4) She will keep a recorder going so she can transcribe the material later; and, finally, (5) She will ask any questions she desires about her mother and others.

Alli would do it right—she'd get to know her mother through these members of The Blue Garter Club. This, indeed, would be a memorable weekend.

The Lakeside Reunion
According to twenty-six-year-old Alli

Thoughts are swirling in Alli's head. Well, this is the
big weekend! Claudia and I traveled the longest distance to attend this event. Ironically, we are the last ones
to arrive at Claudia's cozy cottage on the lake. There are
14 other women—I wonder if they're ready to tell their
stories. Each member welcomed me with a big hug.
Even though these women responded so warmly to me,
I feel a little out of place with this closely-knit group.

While the women are chattering away, I'll pull out
my poster and study the faces. I'll familiarize myself
first with each 1956 face and then with each 1992 face.
I'm surprised to see that many of these women look
very much as they did almost forty years ago. The
women who have gray hair wear it proudly and styl-
ishly; no "dowdy" fifty year olds here. Wrinkles are
few; laughter lines are plentiful; eyes that have cried
many tears are sparkling today.

Claudia told me that I would become best acquainted
with five or six of these women who have intense personal experiences to share. How am I going to ever
remember all 14 women? They are all mothers. All are in
their late fifties. All are white. Most of them are quite
Nordic-looking, and most have a Midwestern accent.
They all seem open and talkative. I'll have to find some
distinctive features to keep them straight in my mind.
I'll jot down some notes for myself:

> There's Barbara, small, trim, perfectly groomed;
> her good looks defy the health problems she has
> had. Her ready smile and giggle describe a delight-
> ful personality. Apparently, she also swings a mean
> golf club. (Barbara=*Golfer*).

> Loquacious Dana, with her quick smile, is an
> instant friend. She is a vocalist, so I will remember
> her as *Ms. Do-Re-Me*. In spite of her husband's death,

her enthusiasm for life is contagious and gives added height to a short stature. She has brown curly hair.

Celia, a former elementary teacher, described herself as a *"domestic engineer."* This tall dark-haired woman will look natural in a square-dancing dress. She and her husband enjoy this activity.

Marilyn, a *pre-school teacher* and musician, is married to a pastor. I will picture her directing a children's choir and teaching little ones. Her slenderness exemplifies the emphasis she places on exercise. Her short gray hair adds distinction.

Laura, a counselor and author, owns a publishing company. Maybe she's a workaholic; she has stayed slim and glamorous over the years. I love the silk jeans she's wearing. I'll identify this blonde lady as a *counselor.*

Aimee has been a vocational education *teacher* for 31 years so I will picture her with computer and steno pad. She is probably the most reserved woman in this group. Watching her now, she seems to be always listening, seldom talking. Her dark brown hair is short.

Sarah, wearing glasses just as she did in college, has this super smile that warms the entire room. Judging from my notes, she's a former teacher who has a variety of interests, including volunteerism. Regular workouts at the gym are also part of her life style. She helped deliver meals on wheels for many years, so maybe I will picture her in that caring capacity for starters...*teacher/ volunteer.*

Kate is a tall, slender widow with short blonde hair, who has her own insurance business. I know she once had a health-food business, and she raised a lot of kids. Kate makes a person feel at ease. To me, she typifies *"Mother Earth."*

Elizabeth, a talented *artist,* will be pictured in my mind with an easel and paints. Perhaps a smock in burgundy would compliment her short gray hair. I wonder what creative wheels are turning in her head for the next canvas.

Renae, married to an ex-military man, is the *world traveler* in the group so I will picture her with a suitcase. She has thick, wavy hair, now gray, that easily falls into place when she runs her fingers through it. Her glasses depict a studious and alert mind in keeping with her desire to see the world.

Audrey looks almost like her college graduation picture. A petite blonde, she even wears the same short hair style she did then. Her warm smile and earnest conversation make me feel very welcome. I will name her *Ms. Hospitality* because my notes indicate that she puts a high priority on entertaining friends in their home.

Sally has this marvelous throaty laugh and sharp wit. Many pictures show her with her head thrown back, mouth wide open, and laughing. She gives a dramatic slant to her speech, gesturing with her hands as she talks, evoking laughter from those around her. She appears warm and friendly, so I'm anxious to know her better. Her brown hair is short, and she's wearing it in a soft curly style. *Ms. Wit* will be her temporary name.

Ann is tall and slender with medium length permed hair. Her choice of words and expressions describe one who has natural acting talent. I know she has acted in plays and industrial videos. An intelligent woman, who is not afraid to take a stand on issues, she served eight years on the city council of a medium-sized Midwestern city. She seems ambitious, competitive, and achievement oriented. I'll call her *Ms. Media*.

Claudia is my friend and neighbor. Her blonde hair has gray highlights giving the illusion of being frosted. She has worked hard on writing this book, so I view her as an organizer, efficient and well prepared. Because she has welcomed me into her life, I know she has a heart of gold. I could identify her as an office manager, but I think I'll promote her to *author*.

I can picture my mother standing in the circle, laughing with these vivacious women. She was beautiful with brown eyes, dark curly hair, and a complexion that needed no make-up. "Oh, how I wish Mother could have been here today!" Alli speaks aloud, though nobody hears her.

I'm amazed that Claudia has handed me the reins as moderator to guide this weekend journey. Claudia shows her generous nature by giving me the sections she'd spent so much time writing in advance of the reunion. I'll review the purposes of this book, as outlined by Claudia.

1) To tell it like it was in 1956.
2) To reminisce about good times, what dorm life was like, courtship, marriage.
3) To share information about how members coped with tough times and heartbreaks in hopes that other people will be encouraged by what they have experienced.
4) To discuss the common thread running through each life—their Christian faith.
5) To encourage women in mid-life to accept new challenges and follow their dreams—to *Go For It!*

I'll make a little bookmark for myself with an alphabetized list of 14 "mind-jogger" names. As much as I've studied these faces, I'm sure that in my excitement I'll lose track of who's who. After a couple days, I'll learn about these multi-dimensional women. But in the meantime, I need a crutch—a "crib list" of sorts.

The Blue Garter Club
Alli's Mind-Jogger

Aimee—*Computer Teacher*
Ann—*Ms. Media*
Audrey—*Ms. Hospitality*
Barbara— *Golf Champ*
Celia—*Domestic Engineer*
Claudia—*The Author*
Dana—*Do-Re-Me*
Elizabeth—*The Artist*
Kate—*Mother Earth*
Laura—*The Counselor*
Marilyn—*Pre-School Teacher*
Renae—*World Traveler*
Sally—*The Wit*
Sarah—*Teacher/Volunteer*

Alli sits back as...

Claudia steps forward as hostess. "We've had a time of informal 'catch up' on the latest news. Now kick off your shoes, sit down, pour a cup of coffee and get ready to talk! I've been working on this book for several months now and have made substantial progress. My heartfelt thanks to each one of you for your written contributions. You've all met Marion's daughter, Alli. Alli, we hope you will feel comfortable with the group that you've been researching the past weeks. I've provided Alli with notes prepared in advance to facilitate laying the groundwork for conversation.

"Recently I've spent so much time thinking about the 1950s that I'd like to refresh your memories about the expectations of the '50s woman. This recollection is probably more for Alli's sake than for the rest of us who were there. Alli, expectations dictated that the primary goal for women was to marry and raise a family. Careers readily available to women were nursing, teaching, and secretarial work. All of us expected to work a little while before starting our families. Perhaps forming The Blue Garter Club was evidence of our acceptance of this social standard. Women's liberation, equal employment opportunities, and minority quotas were not even part of our vocabulary. Concordia's application form for admission contained a question that asked: *'What do you expect to be doing five years after graduation?'* My reply was: 'I expect to be happily married, raising a family.' My prediction came true—after all, this was the 1950s.

"All Blue Garter Club members were prepared for classroom teaching. As graduation neared, our major concerns were twofold: to sign a teaching contract with a good salary ($3,800 top) and to plan our wedding.

"As seniors, several members of The Club were officially engaged to be married, and wedding dates were being set for the summer of '56. Each bride would wear the Blue Garter concealed beneath her wedding dress. I can remember pictures revealing our Blue Garter discreetly displayed when hoisting the skirt to expose the gartered leg. Unless one had legs too skinny to hold it up, the garter was sometimes worn below the knee. Using blue satin and white lace to cover the necessary elastic band, our Blue Garter was a 'one size fits all' variety.

"This will be a strenuous weekend because we have so much territory to cover. It also will have its emotional moments as we recall some of the very tough situations we've been through. Alli has come here to learn more about her mother, what she was like, and what was happening in the '50s that shaped our lives. Alli will be our moderator, allowing me to step out of my author shoes and into my Blue Garter Club membership. My fervent hope is that we will be able to provide material for a book that will not only be interesting, but helpful both to our contemporaries and to Alli's."

1

Dormitory Life...One of the Extras in Extracurricular?

Treasures

*As I walk along the seashore of life
gazing out on waves of despair,
I see a delicate bottle afloat
and watch to see what is there.*

*As slowly it washes up on the beach,
I approach with a cynical eye.
It gleams in the sun and invites me to reach
to open and see what's inside.*

*A treasure I found on the beach that day,
a vessel so full of God's love.
She'd listen to what I had to say,
God sent that friend from above.*

*Yes, to that treasure I could readily pour
my joys and my hurts and my cares.
My friend would accept the pain that I bore,
her compassionate heart she shares.*

*On the beach are vessels of many kinds—
some full, some broken, some bent.
But few are the times when a treasure is found
praise God for the friends He has sent.*

— Lois Qualben

The Blue Garter Club Is Born

Alli picks up the notebook containing Claudia's short history of the Blue Garter Club. Feeling uneasy, she leans forward and begins reading.

"Huddling together, left hands extended, fingers touching the table, we formed a semi-circle around the Blue Garter placed on a piece of royal blue velvet fabric. To identify yourself in this pose— part of a picture-taking session during the creation of The Blue Garter Club—required recognizing your own hand and engagement ring.

"Shortly before college graduation in the spring of 1956, these young women pledged the Blue Garter as a symbol of lasting friendship. Graduation threatened to scatter these friends who had bonded so closely over four years of college. Although not everyone in the group was engaged to be married at this time, expectations included marriage and family. With each member wearing the same Blue Garter at her wedding, we would continue to share in each other's joy even as we went our separate ways. Attired in Sunday best, we organized The Blue Garter Club over dinner in a restaurant's private room.

"We were determined to sweep back the tides that had overwhelmed other college friendship groups before us. We'd grown up in a religious culture that viewed human nature very realistically. Occasional reunions at Homecomings just wouldn't be enough. We needed a symbol and a vehicle to keep us together. So, this Blue Garter became our bonding symbol, since all of us had such a high view of marriage as God's own creation. And, the Round Robin became our vehicle for articulating the diversity and maturing of our ties.

Other groups of graduates have tried to maintain a Round Robin. Too often, they've found it withered away to oblivion. Perhaps the difference for us has been that homemade, simple Blue Garter that Renae had lovingly created for us. As God created for each bride and groom a One New Person, and bonded them to this miracle of a bigger-than-both-of-us Christian marriage, the bride's Blue Garter signified the continued friendship and presence of 14 other women at each wedding. That Blue Garter we wore linked each of us with 14 other miracles like our own. It became a symbol of that creation and a motivation to keep in touch."

Reflections on Four Years of College

"Your stories begin with college life in the early 1950s. Forty years ago, you found each other there. Roommates. Classmates." Alli starts the group's 'engine.' "Please feel free to interrupt or ask questions at any time. I challenge you to ignore this tape recorder I have turned on.

"I want to know why all of you chose this church college, since it cost more than state schools. Why would your families make the financial sacrifice? I think that some religious colleges still charge premium fees for a second-rate education, just so students can continue residence in a religious ghetto. I have learned that Concordia has its distinctive, Nordic-origin, religious values-led culture. But apparently it was—and is—no ghetto." Alli begins to relax and poses the question.

Why did you women choose Concordia?

Celia volunteers. "I chose Concordia because the church school atmosphere seemed more in keeping with what made my family 'work.' When I entered, Mom was a widow. That meant I had to take campus jobs and work summers while attending summer school. Since I majored in elementary education, I completed the minimum two-year program, dropped out my junior year to teach so I could pay for my senior year. Although money had been set aside from my father's estate to educate five children, it was not enough. I also had a second-semester scholarship of $150 for being valedictorian."

Alli gasps. "One hundred fifty dollars wouldn't pay for two of my textbooks these days." She decides not tell about her own $2,500-a-year scholarship.

"Concordia was a natural choice for me because of the church connection. It was close to home, my uncle taught there, and two cousins had been students there," says Sarah. "Family ties."

"I wanted desperately to go to Concordia," says Marilyn, "but my family simply couldn't afford it. After two years at a state school, my dad asked if I still wanted to attend Concordia. My fervent plea brought us to the campus to discuss my transfer. My dad, a strong advocate of higher education for all of his children, devised a scheme whereby he would help his eldest child with tuition, and each child would help the younger siblings with their college expenses. It worked pretty well for our family."

Thinking about her present debt of $12,000 in student loans, Alli asks, "Were student loans as popular then as now?"

Laura answers, "To my knowledge, the student loan program wasn't in existence when we went to college. At least I certainly never heard of a *federal* student loan. When we enrolled in the fall of 1952, tuition was all of $185. The ball-park figure for tuition, fees, room and board for a year was $1,000, which was a lot of money to our parents. Since my dad and sister were Concordia graduates and my mom graduated from St. Olaf in the early 1920s, I had the choice of two colleges. I think all of our parents found it a struggle financially to put us through college. I worked very hard summers to come up with each year's out-of-pocket expenses."

Claudia adds, "I have vivid memories of writing out a check for tuition that first semester. This was the first time I had written a check for such a large amount of money—$185. My hand shook! Here was a timid freshman girl from a small town in North Dakota standing at the window in Old Main writing a $185 check. Wow!"

Alli wonders if anyone besides Celia had a scholarship. Elizabeth runs her fingers through her stylish gray hair and wryly explains, "My high school graduating class had three members! I received a $150 scholarship as salutatorian—the smartest girl in my class. I should add that I was the *only* girl in my class! Although I wasn't Lutheran, a church college atmosphere attracted my mother and brother; they strongly influenced my choice of college."

Smiling, Dana interrupts. "Elizabeth, do you remember how we used to tease you that Concordia must have made an exception in your case, because you were not in the upper one-third of your total graduating class, and generally speaking Concordia only accepted students in that rank!"

With a smile, eyes rolled upward, our resident artist acknowledges the teasing.

Alli presses for our improvisations to pay college expenses in the early '50s. She points to Audrey, that still-small, blonde lady who looks quite the same today as she did on the 1956 picture in Alli's lap.

"Since I was the oldest of six children, our parents had to consider the potential expenses for all of us. Although I stayed out of school the first semester of my senior year to save money, I had enough credits to finish with my class."

Alli glances toward Barbara, a Blue Garter Club member who appears twenty years younger than she is. Alli hopes she looks this good when she's in her late 50s.

Barbara, the Golf Champ, says, "My mother graduated from Concordia in home economics. I followed in her footsteps. From childhood, I just assumed that was my college destiny."

Alli looks around the group and asks, "Is there anyone who did *not* rely on dad or did *not* work summers to finance their college education?"

Claudia peers over her glasses and answers, "Well, actually, I did work summers, but not that earnestly! My education was paid for in a tragic way! My older brother was killed in 1943 in World War II. My mother was named the beneficiary on his GI insurance, and she received a monthly check for $50. She decided that his insurance money would go toward something special. Educating her other children was an utmost priority for her, so she saved those dollars exclusively for college. My brother and I went through college because of her commitment of our lost brother's insurance. And that meant a lot to our motivation to do well."

"Thanks, everyone. I've been living in a sorority house at a tax-supported university, and now I want to know what dormitory life was like for my mother at your church college in the early 1950s."

Now I'm A Co-ed

When referring to her mother, a wave of loneliness overtakes Alli. However, she quickly recovers and focuses on the group. "Can any of you recall your very first day at Concordia?" Sally wasn't laughing now; she mutters something about remembering that day even if she lives to be a hundred.

"I took for granted that I would go to college. My decision to go so far away was a surprise to my parents," starts Sally. "However, they went along with it. Since I wanted to be a teacher, they hoped I would choose a nearby teacher's college. However, I had my heart set on Concordia because several people I really admired spoke so well of it. So I packed up a trunk and several suitcases and traveled by train across North Dakota. Arriving in Moorhead, I called a taxi—a first! The driver helped me haul my trunk and luggage inside the dorm. It seems like yesterday that I dragged those suitcases up two stories and paused in the doorway to survey a pint-sized, sparsely-furnished room. My eyes focused on the beds. *Army cots?* Reality hit me! *Whose idea was it for me to go to college? Why did I choose to leave the comforts of home?"*

Alli says, "I'd probably drag my trunks right back downstairs if that's what I'd encountered at the University.

Sarah recalls, "Barbara and I were roommates. When we arrived that first day, we dumped all of our things in the middle of the floor and went to a movie. Later that evening, we unpacked and went to work on our room. There was a 'tap tap' at the door, and the housemother told us we were making too much noise for so late in the evening! Reprimanded, very first day!!"

Alli shakes her head and seems incredulous. "Was it really *that* strict?" She continues reading from the prepared manuscript.

First Assignment: *Memorize The Rules*

"Freshmen women entering in the fall of 1952 were immediately introduced to 'The Rules.' We had to be back in the dorm by 7:30 week nights and 10:00 on weekends! Women were allowed one late night during the week. If a student signed out for an evening of studying at the library, that was counted as a 'night out.' This policy didn't encourage many evenings at the library."

Laura interjects: "My sister graduated just before I enrolled. When she told me that freshmen women had to be in by 7:30, I thought she was just kidding me. What a blow to settle into the dorm that first week and find out she was telling it like it was!" Alli can't believe this. Remembering the stories her grandmother told about her fun-loving mother, she surmised that her mom must have hated "The Rules."

Alli continues reading from Claudia's prepared manuscript.

"The Rules stipulated evening quiet hours for studying. Devotions were held in the dormitory lounges at 9:30 every night, and lights were turned off at 10:30. Before 'lights out,' floor proctors conducted a bed check to determine that everyone was accounted for. When the lights blinked, we knew we had another ten minutes before they went off. Many of us suffered eyestrain from studying by flashlight."

Sally interrupts. "Trying to make a dorm room cozy was a real challenge for us. We had a corner room on the second floor, with a window visible from the street. To brighten up our room, we bought a red shade for the desk lamp. Naive as we were, we thought nothing of having this red light in our window—until we noticed it drew at lot of attention and laughter from male students. There were no red light districts in our small home towns!"

Alli continues reading from the prepared script.

"Living with so many women under one roof was new to all of us. It took some getting used to— we had to share, help each other, and be considerate. Each dormitory had a house mother whose job was to keep dormitory life free from catastrophes, other than academic sorts. Since most of us were living away from home for the first time, we learned new skills—like clothes washing. Clothes racks, clothes lines, and a wringer-type washing machine with rinse tubs were available in each dormitory base-

ment. Although automatic washers and dryers were on the market, they were not yet commonplace. Certainly not in our dormitory!"

Alli's big brown eyes opened wide in disbelief. She continues.

"A catastrophe was when too much bluing caused our white underwear to turn blue, or too much bleach streaked a colored blouse. It also was a catastrophe if you forgot to sign up for the washing machine. Some of us avoided such risks by sending our laundry home to Mom. When the laundry box came back, invariably there'd be a package of homemade cookies tucked in with the clothes. Happiness meant clean clothes and Mom's homemade chocolate chip cookies.

"Each dorm had a modestly-equipped kitchenette. Coke was bottled in six-ounce bottles; cans had not yet come into their own as soft drink containers. No candy or pop vending machines were available. You could buy candy in the dorm from students who took turns as candy vendors."

Alli quickly grabs for a cold Coke on the table, perhaps fearful that these women will remove it in favor of some old-fashioned drink like iced tea.

Laura remembers her stint at selling candy. "During our freshman year, Audrey and I were elected Dorm Candy Chairmen. That meant we were in charge of ordering candy, scheduling students to sell candy each evening, taking care of the money, and then storing the candy stock underneath our army cots. Our skirts got tighter and tighter. Don't you remember what weight problems freshmen girls had, even without candy beckoning from under the bed?" Heads nod in remembrance.

"Things haven't changed much on that score," Alli chimes in as she observes this slender lady who doesn't quite fit the image of an undisciplined candy gobbler.

Alli continues. *"College personnel made a sin-
cere effort to match up the freshmen women who
would, they hoped, be compatible and happy living
together in such confined quarters. The freshman
dorm rooms contained beds, dressers, desks and
chairs, along with a 'too-small' closet. A light bulb
dangled from the ceiling. The centrally-located com-
munal bathrooms, which turned into Grand Central
Station before 8:00 a.m. classes, provided no privacy. Hot rollers were non-existent; curling irons
and blow-dry hair styles were rare. Instead, night-
time rituals included rolling one's hair on uncomfortable curlers. Girls who needed only a few bobby
pins were envied."*

Aimee comments, "We were all envious of Marion's
natural wave and easy wash-and wear hair style."

Alli gasps, *"No hot rollers?* What are curlers anyway?"

Smiling tolerantly, the women chose to ignore her.
"The upper-class dorm had beautiful rooms for either
three or four women. Based upon completion of Friendship 101, sophomores, juniors, and seniors chose their
own roommates," Audrey adds.

"One of the luxuries which the upper-class women
enjoyed was a sink in each room, which alleviated most
bathroom lines," Elizabeth remembers.

"Sinks were not enough! We needed showers in
each dorm room!" snarls Sally with an expression of
mock indignation. "Can you imagine what it's like to be
down the hall in the shower, and these so-called 'friends'
sneak in and remove your towel, bathrobe and slippers,
leaving absolutely nothing!" Sally gestures to describe
her predicament, making everyone laugh as they remember. "And then they opened the door at the end of
the hallway, so anyone entering the front door of the
dorm could see all the way down the hall!"

"We left you a few things to wear, didn't we?"

"Oh, sure! Earrings and snow boots! A lot of good that did!"

By now everyone is enjoying a hearty laugh at Sally's recollection. "Well, we did finally give you a towel and a sweater, because I remember we also took a picture."

Now completely relaxed, Alli joins Sally's infectious laughter.

Dana comments, "It was great fun playing jokes on Sally because she was so good natured. Sally, I remember another time you were the object of a joke. Alli, are you familiar with Norwegian *lefse?*"

"Yes, I think so. It looks like a tortilla, doesn't it?"

Sally gestures toward the culprits and explains, "Right. When we were freshmen, someone received a package of lefse from home. We spread butter on the lefse, sprinkled sugar on it and rolled it up. A lefse was prepared for me; everyone seemed unusually interested in watching me eat it, quizzing me as to how I liked it. I said it was really good. Afterwards, I learned that they had rolled up a single Kleenex tissue inside the lefse, which I ate and didn't even know it!" Sally lets out a hoot with everyone else.

"I imagine you were allowed to leave campus *once in a while,*" Alli says sarcastically. "How did you get down town? Were there city buses?"

Laura explains, "Alli, quite unlike colleges today, Concordia didn't allow women students to have a car on campus. Occasionally an upper-classman might have a car available for a short term, but walking was the most popular mode of transportation, regardless of weather. Since dressing up for church was the custom, we walked in high heels for six blocks to get there. After church we usually trudged downtown to eat dinner at a favorite cafe. Since stores were closed on Sundays, there were no 'warm up' stops on our penetratingly cold walk back to the dormitory. On those coldest Sundays in Minnesota, the backs of our legs turned white by the time we reached our destination. Frost bite. Why didn't we take a bus? Buses didn't run on Sundays, or if they did, they were few and far between.

"In those days it was unacceptable for women to wear slacks to church, and slacks were forbidden in our classrooms. Slacks could be worn on campus on Saturdays, but not to Saturday classes."

"Didn't you ever roll your slacks up beyond your coat line?" asks Barbara with a grin. "That worked in an emergency! If you overslept!"

Audrey adds. "Skirts, saddle shoes and bobby socks were appropriate classroom attire. Many women wore nylons and dress shoes. Since the idea of pantyhose hadn't yet been conceived, our nylons were held in place by you-know-what—yes, girdles!!"

Alli gulps, *"No pantyhose?"*

"How did we ever survive sitting through all those classes wearing girdles?" someone whines.

"We were skinny then!" says Kate. "Wearing shorts on campus was absolutely forbidden except for physical education classes. Students had to change into their shorts at the gymnasium and back into their street clothes after class."

Alli looks down at Claudia's prepared notes and continues.

Here I am... *Where's the Social Life?*

"Campus social events in the early 1950s were closely regulated. A freshman picnic was part of the fall social calendar. Because someone figured it was time to match up these young men and women, the administration came up with some contrivances that seem ludicrous today. For instance, after everyone had assembled in the dorm, our house mother called out the names of two freshmen—one man and one woman. These two stepped forward to meet, and then walked together to the picnic in the park. Match-

ing up a whole freshman class this way produced a long line of couples walking for several blocks. Passers-by must have wondered about this strange parade—was Noah's Ark getting loaded?"

"I remember that picnic! Who was my date? I can't remember who I went with!" laughs Dana shaking her head. Alli steps back into the spotlight and continues.

"One social event at the beginning of fall semester was called the 'Shakathon.' The freshmen formed a huge circle on the gym floor, and the older students walked inside the circle shaking hands with the freshmen. When upper-classmen had come full circle, they formed an inner circle to greet each other as well.

"Social dancing on Concordia's campus wasn't allowed in the early 1950s. We did have parties where square dancing was enjoyed, but we had to call it 'square games.' Although dates were not required for attending these affairs, boy-meets-girl gimmicks were part of the scene when each girl removed one of her shoes and added it to a pile in the middle. Each fellow picked up a shoe and, once he found 'Cinderella,' he had a partner for the next round of square games. More than a few students felt that the name 'square games' described what kind of people took part in that activity."

Laura interrupts. "I suspect students of the '90s would have very soon discovered the Crystal Ballroom. You could get expelled from Concordia for going there. When Louie Armstrong performed at the Crystal, several of us thought it was worth the risk to hear 'Satchmo.' Alli, your mom was part of that outing. She loved jazz, you know. Needless to say, we kept a very low profile!" Laura looks at an accomplice who nods her head saying, "Ohhh yes!"

A glance around the group reveals 14 smiling women who enjoy reminiscing as they listen to the extracted notes of those early days in college. Alli reads the narrative's next heading.

I'm Still Here... *Where's the Social Life?*

> *"The dormitory setting fostered our friendships throughout four years. Despite an avalanche of those early 1950's restrictions, we didn't feel persecuted. Little did we know that the 7:30 p.m. hours would make wonderful conversational fodder in years to come, especially when our own daughters felt parental rules were too confining."*

Fourteen 'same-age' mothers agreed to that! Alli continues reading.

> *"Anyway, things changed the following year when a new Dean of Women came. Complaints about the dull social life on campus didn't go unheeded. Apparently the 'powers that be' felt obligated to encourage dating. The new Dean of Women tried to impress upon the male students the high caliber of Concordia's female students. She said something like: 'I think you will find that the women on this campus stack up well against the women on any other campus.' The men, of course, found this statement amusing since they had their own definition of 'well stacked.'*
> *"In spite of complaints about the dull social life, dating did occur. On weekends, dorm entrances were filled with smooching couples. At 10:00 p.m., a certain house mother was always watering the plants in the lounge near the entrance. This gave her an excuse to keep a sharp eye on the avid activities happening in our vestibule. Since the vestibule was filled to capacity with about a half-dozen snuggling*

couples standing shoulder to shoulder in their heavy storm coats, the need for oxygen could supplant affectionate impulses. As the clock struck 10:00, a final good-night kiss and a hasty push toward the closing door was a frequent outcome."

"*Vestibule?* What on earth is a vestibule?" Alli laughs.

"It was the *passion pit,* Alli, and I remember your mom doing her share of snuggling in the *vestibule,*" quips Sally in her typically animated expression. "Remember how mortifying it was to have to ring the bell if we arrived late? Hands on her hips, the house mother would lay a heavy lecture and impose a few demerits which could lead to being 'campused.'" Sally's imitation extracts laughter, as the others remember their own experiences. Alli returns to Claudia's notes.

> *"But a Saturday night without a date wasn't a sentence of death because the college had invested in a black and white television set for the upper-class dormitory lounge. Fellows and gals could be informal as they watched the 'Hit Parade' and made popcorn in the nearby kitchenette."*

Alli shakes her head and looks at the group. "No color TV?" She glances down at the next heading, and lets out another gasp!

One Phone for the Entire Dorm?

> *"Telephones in the dormitories were few and far between in the early 1950s. A phone on each floor was typical for the upper-class dorm; but one phone served the entire freshman dorm. Each resident had to take her turn on 'phone duty,' which meant taking messages during evening quiet hours."*

Sally interrupts. "My parents would write and tell me that they'd call me on a certain night, and since

telephones weren't used for long distance as much as
they are today, I waited anxiously for those calls. But as
soon as I heard their voices, I started to cry and for three
or four minutes I couldn't talk—only cry. I was terribly
homesick, extremely unhappy for the first months of
my freshman year. It must have been so hard on my
parents to hear me sobbing and talking about transfer-
ring to the teacher's college close to home. They didn't
go for that idea at all. Traveling home meant riding by
train all the way across North Dakota. The only times
we went home were for summer, Thanksgiving, Christmas, and Easter."

Alli empathizes with Sally, "I'd be unhappy, too, if
someone was rolling up Kleenex in my lefse!" She looks
down at Claudia's notebook and smiles as she announces
the next topic.

Of Vice and Men

> "Opportunities to get acquainted with the men
> students occurred through classes, labs, choir, band,
> social gatherings, and even chapel. Since the college
> had a mandatory chapel attendance policy, we had
> assigned seats so attendance could be taken. Al-
> though sororities and fraternities weren't allowed at
> Concordia, 'societies' were very much a part of
> campus life—each with its own unique reputation."

"To this day, our two Concordia-grad children fret
over the fact I belonged to a 'society' which *now* has a
notorious party reputation," Laura muses. Smiling, Alli
continues.

> "The societies were quite competitive. Some bit-
> ter tears were shed when freshmen pledges were
> turned down by their chosen society. Nonetheless,
> social life was expanded through sister-brother Soci-

ety occasions. Remember the great variety shows we used to put on?

"If caught consuming alcohol, suspension from Concordia was immediate. Smoking on campus was also forbidden for women. Nevertheless, a few tales are told of occasional puffs of smoke being exhaled through three little holes at the bottom of the dormitory storm windows, wafting into the cold, crisp night air above. Someone claimed it was only 'Holy Smoke' announcing the selection of a new Pope."

Alli interjects, "The most verbal opponents of smoking at the dorms and sorority houses at the U. are the health-conscious students who wage war on people who smoke in their space. Did my mom smoke?"

"No, Alli, she didn't. But at church colleges in the '50s, smoking was considered more a 'sin' than a health hazard. Of course there was a double standard. It wasn't sinful for *men* to smoke! However, there was no talk back then of smoking as a cause of cancer or heart disease," Renae comments.

Determined to complete this prepared history in a timely manner, Alli asserts herself and continues reading.

Dormitory Parties and Pictures Abound

"Our photo albums can vouch for our frequent dorm parties. Snapshots show us clad in pajamas and housecoats, the usual garb for relaxation. One year we purchased matching baby-doll pajamas. We felt pretty risque when we took a cheesecake picture of the whole group with their bare shoulders and legs wearing those 'Teddys' of the 50s."

"I think we all have that picture in our albums," says Kate. Others smile and nod.

"Hey, we didn't look half bad!" Sally laughs as Alli returns to Claudia's notes.

"Sharing was a big part of dormitory life. Clothes. Food from home. We shared not only divinity and popcorn, but we shared our joys, our anxieties, our hopes and our dreams. This sharing contributed to lasting friendships."

I Heard a Scream. *Who's Engaged?*

"One of the greatest joys we had to share with our friends was getting engaged. Returning to the dormitory after that very special evening with him and showing off a diamond engagement ring was a highlight of dorm life. A newly-engaged student need only wave her third finger, left hand, to trigger loud screams from those around her. The 'Diamond Scream' brought other dorm women running to the source to admire the ring and to join in the glory of the moment. This was the standard method for communicating to the entire dormitory that someone had become engaged."

"In a women's dorm today, a scream like that would make someone dial 911," suggests Alli.

Exploring education or hunting a husband?

Sally comments, "Considering society's view of women in the 1950s, a lot of people thought getting a husband was the main reason we went to college!"

Sarah speaks up: "Young women were under tremendous pressure in those days to find a husband who was getting a college education. I certainly felt that pressure. Being a single career woman was *not* a desirable option!!"

"Wait a minute! Not only did I not feel that pressure," exclaims Renae, the World Traveler, "I deliberately planned to focus on my career. For me, marriage waited for seven years after we graduated." She laughs. "Now you know who packed away our Blue Garter!"

"I agree. Many of our classmates weren't engaged at graduation time," says Celia. "College prepared me to teach and that's what I did for several years before I met my husband. There were times when I even fantasized that I would return to Concordia as a faculty member— *if* I didn't get married!"

Aimee, the computer teacher, adds, "As seniors, many of you were either engaged or getting serious, but a few of us were totally unattached. If a diamond ring was a requirement for membership in the Blue Garter Club, I would have been rejected! Four years went by before I changed my name."

This diversity was not what Alli expected. Alli exclaims: "Husband-hunting stereotypes certainly do not fit this Club. So, there were two rungs at the top of the priority ladder—getting a quality education no less than finding a suitable husband. It sounds to me that the caliber of your education really was the more important of the two." Sensing no dissent from her observation, Alli reads a concluding sentence.

"The Blue Garter Club was born. Now, 36 years later, our combined experiences could fill a book! This book!"

Alli looks down at her mother's senior picture and feels her mother's presence. "I'm so grateful to share these memories. I'll learn so much about my mother through you 14 women who were once so close to her. I can hardly wait to hear more about courtship in the '50s, your views on husbands and marriage, and your first homes."

2

"Oh, Please...Don't Call Eve a Spare Rib!"

Housework

I love to cook,
I love to sew,
I love to scrub the floor;
I figure if I say it enough
I'll learn to love it more.

I love to wash the diapers,
*   they're as sweet as sweet can be.*
A housewife has a glamorous task,
*   just ask your hubby and see.*

Did you ever stop to figure your pay,
*   just about a dime a day!*
Go tell him to get another slave—
*   then listen to him rant and rave.*

He'll say he provides you with meat and drink,
*   he'll pout or put up a real stink;*
*   he'll tell you you're lucky as lucky can be,*
*   to have a spouse as delightful as he.*

> *He thinks he gives you a real break*
> *   when he drags in for supper at half past eight.*
> *If he only knew how much sweat and strain*
> *   it took to open that frozen chow mein.*

— Lois Qualben

"Before we get into demands of housework and kids, a discussion of courtship and first homes is forthcoming," Alli says as she turns on the recorder.

"It all started with Adam and Eve. According to the Bible, God caused a deep sleep to come over Adam. Then God took a portion of the man's rib to make a woman, a helpmate for man." Alli pauses. "Isn't that amazing? God makes such a magnificent creature—the first real woman—from such inferior resources! First, Adam out of dust; now, this! It must have become a habit, given the way God still creates Christians."

Sally laughs and says, "We've already come to treasure your casual insights, Alli."

"The first part of this chapter on husbands will be light-hearted—light and fluffy. I'm with a group of women who represent nearly 500 years of marriage—notice I did not say 'marital bliss.' The longevity of your marriages speaks for itself."

"Well, everyone knows the first 500 years are the hardest!" someone blurts out.

"Was that Mrs. Methuselah?"

Elizabeth asks, "You want this chapter to be light and fluffy? As in: Omelets? If we talk too much, will we end up with egg on our face?"

Sarah says, "Our husbands were raised in a time that assumed an innate superiority for males, based on the claim that since God made man first, a woman should remember her second-place status."

"But we can insist that God saved the best till last—that making Adam was only a practice run," Barbara laughs. "And since man was made from dust, that helpmate assignment for Eve meant she had to keep the dust under control," adds Celia. "That would certainly make women superior...according to the Bible."

"The story I heard about Adam," starts Audrey, "is that he was not quite prepared for this 'helpmate' relationship. After spending some time getting acquainted with Eve, he sought out God for some answers. He first asks, 'What is a hug?' God gives him an answer. Then he asks, 'What is a kiss?' God tells him. Adam goes back to Eve. Next time he talks to God, he has another question. 'What is a headache?'"

Steering us back, Alli says, "From books I've seen on Christian relationships, recent research has pretty much overridden such hierarchical misinterpretations of what the Bible teaches about male-female relationships. But, now, Laura, start us off with some courtship stories—what it was like in the '50s."

Insights into Courtship—1955 Style

Mr. Right Sometimes Came from Far-Away Places

"I met my future husband on a blind date," starts Laura. "During the summer of '55, I worked as a lifeguard at a church-related camp out East and fell in love with upstate New York. So, at Homecoming that fall, I overlooked the fact that Jack was a seminary student when a mutual friend suggested a blind date with this New Yorker. We double dated with those friends who had 'fixed us up.'

"Jack's first glimpse of his future wife was of me playing in the concert band. Remember what we wore? Those long black dresses?

"On our second date that weekend, we went canoeing on the Red River. It was in flood stage, and there had been a recent drowning in that part of the river. It should have been no laughing matter when this novice New York tipped our canoe in the middle of the river, but I almost drowned from uncontrollable nervous laughter. Jack had only one really nice wool outfit his parents bought for him just before he left for seminary. He was wearing it—in the water!"

Alli urges Laura to continue. "Minnesota girl meets and marries New York City boy: That match verges on what we call 'Multi-cultural' today! Tell us more, Laura."

"Jack and I continued our long-distance (250 miles one way) romance between Luther Seminary and our campus.

"'Mr. Cool' drove between St. Paul and Moorhead in his mellow yellow convertible which unfortunately was missing several important items—like a working heater. Not wise for Minnesota winters! Some of his gas station stops were to buy oil rather than to fill the gas tank; that car burned a gallon of oil each way. To share expenses on these trips, Jack usually had some passengers— fellow seminary students who also had romantic interests at Concordia. Before returning to seminary one 30-below-zero night, Jack tried to scrape the snow and frost off the plastic rear window and…the whole thing shattered. For 250 miles back to Minneapolis, one of his two riders sat wrapped in a blanket—with only his nose visible. Trying to keep warm, the other seminarian (an exchange student from India) rocked back and forth singing songs of hope and comfort—in Hindi. But from then on, nobody would travel with Jack to Moorhead.

"Jack had gone to barber school on the Bowery, figuring he could earn money cutting 600-plus male heads of hair at seminary. When he was out of money, he'd advise both students and faculty they really needed haircuts (for $1). He usually made enough for gas (28 cents a gallon), oil, and a hamburger with me."

Audrey commented, "You were surprised to learn that Jack's mother was a North Dakota native."

"Yes. Jack's parents had lived in New York City for twenty years, but his mother knew that 'God has sent a girl for Jack' when she found out I was born in Hatton—the same little town in North Dakota where she was born and raised! My father had been the school superintendent when her youngest sisters were in school. This may seem like coincidence, a small-world-after-all kind of thing. But far too many unlikely ingredients came together just right for it to be anything but God's recipe."

Beware: The Vets Are Returning

"Remember how we were warned about the veterans who were coming back to college after the Korean War? As you all know, I married one of them!" says Do-Re-Me. "Chris and I had our first date on Leap Year Day. While we were in the movie theatre, police towed away his car because he had parked in the wrong spot. We had to walk in snow and ice to the police station to get the car back, and, of course, Chris got a ticket. I never let him live it down."

"I also married one of those vets," starts Sally, "and the Dean of Women summoned a few of us to her office for a warning. In a round-about way, she implied that these vets had experienced 'who knows what' and might be expecting more than just a casual date with a nice Christian girl. We couldn't wait to leave her office so we could laugh. Now with our daughter at Concordia, I view that Dean's concern much differently than I did then.

"Paul and I had been dating during part of my junior year when I went home for Christmas vacation. I liked him, but was not yet smitten. He wanted to meet my folks, and I remember spending a half hour on the phone trying to discourage him from coming. I felt his meeting my parents was so final, that it meant we would *have* to get engaged, and I was not ready for that. Read my lips—I was not going to get married right out of college. Anyway, dad walked by the phone and said, 'If he wants to come, let him come.' So I relented. Shortly after vacation was over, mother wrote to tell me how much they liked Paul. It was like a big green light was on! We were engaged the next fall and yes, I did get married right out of college, after all."

"It sounds like your parents' approval was very important to you," suggests Alli. "I don't think most of my friends place parental approval high on their list of priorities—at least, they wouldn't admit it. On the other hand, you women had—and have—such a high view of marriage and family that I'm not surprised."

"Yes, my parents' approval was very important to me. My first meeting with Paul's parents was pretty funny. His parents were true-blue Lutherans and Republicans. They assumed I was Lutheran because of our college. But figuring out whether our family was Republican was more difficult. Paul's dad finally asked what kind of work my dad did. I told him that he's a pharmacist who has a drug store. He said, 'Oh, he's in business for himself. Then he must be a Republican!' I answered, 'Yes, as a matter of fact he is.' From that point on, the tension was eased and I was 'in.'"

College Matrimonial Bureaus Have Many Doors

"I met my husband because of our college's mandatory chapel attendance policy," Claudia recalls. "Do you remember how we had assigned seats in the gym and someone always took attendance? Sally and I signed up to sit together, and my future husband and his friends chose the seats next to us. It must have been some of God's doing because no special thought went into choosing those particular seats. I never did find out what the punishment was for missing chapel because I was strongly motivated to attend!"

"My future husband and I played in the concert band's trumpet section," says Barbara, the Golfer. Alli marvels that this attractive lady is not only a golf champ, but she's a musician, too. "He was at one end of the row, and I was at the other end. When the band went on tours, Laura and I always roomed together and would compare notes on which men in band would be a good 'catch.' John met one of my 'catch' criteria—he had a car! Anyway, we started dating on concert band tours.

"Since John was on the college golf team, many weekends he was out of town for golf meets. One of those weekends there was a society banquet I wanted desperately to attend. Laura lined me up with a date. I was living off campus in an apartment with Sarah. While I told John about my banquet plans, he was bouncing a golf ball. Although he said nothing, his real feelings came through loud and clear. He kept bouncing that golf ball harder and higher, until he missed a catch and the ball shattered the ceiling light."

"So, you realized that your plans had you in hot water with John, and you would soon be in hot water with your landlord for breaking a light fixture," Alli noted.

"Right. It did put a strain between John and me, but I went to that society banquet. Laura and I were pretty good at conniving," adds Barbara, smirking at Laura.

Alli says, "I haven't met anyone I'd be interested in marrying, so I'm finding these stories fascinating. Kate, how did you meet your husband?"

Kate answers. "Take notes on this, Alli. I was 'pushy' enough to introduce myself to him. I remembered Dan from Bible Camp and knew that he lived 15 miles from my home town. How convenient for catching rides home! I suppose he was taken aback by my boldness when I stopped him on campus, called him by name, and introduced myself. He asked me for a date during

Christmas vacation and then offered me a ride back to school. I left my snow boots in his car, so he had to return them to me. For years, Dan insisted I'd left them there deliberately. I was thrilled to be dating him. He was half Icelandic, half Norwegian, 6 foot 3, and *gorgeous!*"

"Actually, Kate, 6 foot 3 and *gorgeous* is good reason to remember any guy from Bible Camp!" Elizabeth teases.

Sadie Hawkins strikes again

Marilyn speaks up. "With Kate's help, I met my husband, Jerome, on a blind date during Sadie Hawkins Week. As a junior transfer student majoring in elementary education, I didn't know many male students. Alli, your mom wanted to go out with Bob, a friend of Jerome's. She decided she'd ask Bob to attend a campus concert, if I'd ask Jerome. Not even knowing who Jerome was, I called him. He accepted. Marion asked Bob, but he already had a date. Now...I had a date. But she didn't! I wasn't too keen about going out alone with someone I'd never seen before, so Kate came to my rescue and asked someone. Sticking with the Sadie Hawkins Week tradition, we trudged over to Jerome's apartment, to the concert, and later downtown for dessert. Today, even high school kids claim they must have wheels because 'he who walks, walks *alone*.' How different it was for us!"

Alli comments, "My friends are reluctant to go out with strangers now with all the problems of date rape, drugs, and drinking. But, your blind date led to a longer relationship."

"Indeed it did. I graduated a year ahead of Jerome, and I taught in the Fargo Public Schools while he completed his senior year. Later we were married. But your mother never did date Bob, Alli."

Nearly Neighbors

"I met my future husband in first grade, and we went through grades one through twelve together!" Sarah says. "He's an only child, and I'm an only child. I've read that this is one of the most difficult matches for a good marriage. I don't disagree!"

"I married a man from my home town, too," adds Audrey, "and now we have come full circle. After living in several other states, we've moved back to retire in the countryside village where both of us grew up. We were introduced at a high school alumni Christmas gathering in the '50s. Art and I discovered we were both from large families and our parents were friends. We realized our ideals, values, and hopes for the future were the same. We fell in love. During our courtship, Art was in school in Minneapolis, and I was at Concordia, so we wrote letters to each other every day. That was common practice at that time, but now phone calls are our kids' way of keeping in touch."

"You're right. I don't know anybody who writes honest-to-goodness love letters anymore." Alli looks around with raised eyebrows.

Ann is pleasantly succinct. "I was in graduate school in Denver, but I also married someone from back home, someone I had known in high school. We never dated in high school, but we were in a play together. I remember his last line was: 'Eileen, will you marry me?' And my line was: 'I've been meaning to all along.'"

"A 'staged' marriage," Alli grins and gets a good laugh. Then she adds, "My mom and dad were high school sweethearts back in Minneapolis."

Flexibility Pays Off

"I met my husband because of the Asian flu," Celia begins. "I was one of several new teachers in town, and

Gene was a new engineer. Gene wanted to meet some of the new teachers, so a friend arranged for my roommate to meet him. She got Asian flu the day they were to meet, so I was her replacement. I had just gotten over the flu."

Kate asks ever-so sweetly, "Did God lead you to your husband-to-be by controlling the timing of who got the Asian flu and when?"

"So you were second string? A substitute? You moved up from second fiddle?" teases Sally.

"Flexibility pays off," Celia says with a smile.

"And they square danced happily forever after," Alli laughs. "This is great. Maybe there's hope for me yet!"

The World Traveler says, "I was teaching in my future husband's home town. I met him at a party while he was home on leave from the Air Force. A week after we met he went back, but we corresponded. See, Alli—another writer of love letters. When school was out, I went to Hawaii, and he was sent to Morocco. Our courtship continued by mail. Before meeting Jerry, marriage was not a concern of mine. At that time, a woman of 22 was considered an 'old maid,' so I was getting used to that label from my cousins. More important to me was the prospect of traveling and seeing the world."

The artist is next. "Ours is a classic example of 'fixing up friends.' I was dating Don's friend. His friend and I arranged a double date with Don and one of my women friends. But, then, Don and I started dating, and within three months we were married."

"Can we include some memorable wedding episodes about plans for a storybook wedding that ended up with at least one very noticeable 'typo' on the page?" Alli asks.

A Gift-Giving Occasion

Barbara interrupts. "Before we move on to our weddings, do you remember how our group had special parties when one of us got engaged? We'd go to the Rex Cafe for a nice dinner, and we would give the bride-to-be a gift. I received a lovely black Fostoria bowl for my engagement present. I still have it."

"Your Fostoria bowl is nearing antique status about now, isn't it?" Sarah speaks up. "I think these engagement parties really got The Blue Garter Club started. After several of them, we started discussing our wedding plans. That's when someone came up with the idea that each one of us wear the same blue garter on our wedding day. Renae volunteered to sew the garter before our next party. Although it seemed like a neat idea, we didn't know it would symbolize such a lasting bond and nearly four decades of writing our Round Robin letters."

"The Blue Garter idea was inspired," says Alli. "I've seen the picture of my mother wearing the blue garter, but until now I didn't know so many of you wore the same one. Now...I want to hear about those typos on your storybook weddings."

Storybook Weddings With a "Typo" or Two

Claudia points her finger at Kate. "Kate is the 'typo' on my storybook wedding page! She was supposed to be one of my bridesmaids, but she didn't get there in time for the wedding service, just the reception."

"What happened?" asks Alli.

Kate answers in her own defense. "Dan's father had died that week, and the funeral was held on Saturday. So we couldn't set out for Claudia's wedding until early Sunday morning. We ran into a lot of construction and poorly-marked roads as we drove all the way across North Dakota. Unfamiliar with Claudia's territory, we overlooked a sign and we had to double back. Finally we arrived at the church after Claudia's wedding service was in progress. The ladies serving the reception in the church basement showed me where to change into my bridesmaid dress. I waited in the entrance until the wedding was over, and then I slipped into the reception line with everyone else. The funny thing was that only one guest seemed to realize I hadn't been up in front with the others."

Claudia recalls, "When the service ended, Martin and I walked down the aisle, and I saw Dan standing in the back, grinning. Wedding excitement must have sent my mind into the ozone because seeing this man somehow made me relieved and happy. But I couldn't remember who he was!"

Celia says, "At our storybook wedding, the 'typo' was Gene's voice. He was ready to repeat his vows, and he lost his voice! Maybe it was nerves. Suddenly he was hoarse."

"Oh sure! Or was it that he finally realized what he was doing, and it scared him speechless?" Sally laughs.

"At our wedding ceremony, the officiating pastor was probably more nervous than either the bride or groom," begins Laura. "He was newly ordained and ours was his first wedding. Not only was the groom a future pastor, but there were three pastors in the wedding party plus Jack's mother, a pastor's wife. Thirty years later, this man still remembers our wedding!"

Honeymoons To Exotic Places?

"Our honeymoon was *real* exotic—a camping trip. We had everything packed and ready to go before the wedding," says Dana. "But when Chris' friends found our hidden camping gear, they proceeded to tear the labels off all our canned goods and load the car with rice. So for the entire week, rice was coming out of absolutely everything—rice in the floorboards, rice in the rugs, rice everywhere!"

"Every meal was rice gumbo and the mystery dish!" Sally chuckles.

"Don and I spent our wedding night at our new home, which until then was 'his' place," begins Elizabeth. "Unknown to us, Don's brother, his best man, had gotten a key. The whole family showed up that night for a shivaree. They also took labels off our canned goods, including the dog food. Their shenanigans did not endear his family to me for a long time!!"

Celia reminisces. "We left frozen Minnesota and spent two weeks at Miami Beach! This was my first experience flying. It was wonderful. So wonderful that I got pregnant on our honeymoon. We had our first baby exactly nine months after the wedding."

"We headed for Glacier Park but never did get there," says Claudia. "Martin got sick with an awful cold. He was in such misery that we cut our honeymoon short and returned home after stopping at a doctor's office for medication. We were gone just a few days."

"And what did the doctor recommend? Bed rest?" asks Elizabeth, with a twinkle in her eye.

Marilyn recalls their honeymoon trip. "Jerome and I cleaned up our car before we left on the trip. But we never checked for Limburger cheese on the manifold! That odor permeated our car for months afterward— every time we started the engine. In fact, when I got pregnant a few months after our wedding, the smell of Limburger cheese worsened my nausea and morning sickness!"

Laughing at Marilyn's expression of disgust at smelling Limburger cheese, Alli asks for stories about our first homes.

Home Sweet Home: Love Nest for Two

"Our first home was a furnished one-bedroom house we rented for $55 a month," says Sarah. "You could call it a bungalow, but that sounds much too generous! The bathroom was in the dirt floor basement. A wood stove heated that bath and the kitchen. Pointing to the stack of wood in the garage, our landlord seemed proud that the rent included all the wood we could burn! The living room was heated with an oil burner. Soon after we moved in, we had a chimney fire and had to call the fire department.

"The laundry? We had to set up our machine and tubs in the kitchen. Guess how many times we washed clothes that way? Once did it," continued Sarah holding up one finger. "There were no laundromats in town, but several women took in laundry. Mid-year when we switched to a different lady, we caused hard feelings." With a sigh she adds, "Life in a small town!"

Alli shakes her head. "I gotta say, I'm glad times are different. Maybe I'm just a 'wimp!'"

Dana smiles at Alli: "Alli, we lived in a house with a basement foundation so full of cracks you could see all the way up town! Eventually we got a new basement. Construction created a sea of mud in the yard where Micky, our over-sized Weimaraner, played. What a mess! Micky soon learned to wait by the door so I could wash his feet; he would lift first one paw and then the other to have them washed off. I was pregnant, so it was a chore to bend over to wash the dog's feet! The house was terrible, but life was wonderful! I think we paid $25 a month rent."

"And all the wood you could burn?" laughs Celia.

A True Vine-Covered Cottage

"Our first home in New Mexico was truly a vine-covered cottage located behind the home of a lovely older couple," begins the World Traveler, "but with vines covering one entire wall of our home, we also had lots of spiders! When Jerry was sent to Germany, we had a fifth-floor apartment. There were no elevators. The kitchen was about 4 feet by 6 feet furnished with a tiny refrigerator, but no oven. Not to worry, this apartment was conveniently located over a bakery! Andy was a baby during our stay here, and I lugged the stroller, the baby, and my packages up and down five flights of stairs. Daily shopping is the custom in Europe."

Shared Bathrooms

"Our first home in Minneapolis was one room upstairs in a rather sleazy house," starts Laura, "but the price was right—$35 a month! The couch turned into a two-part rollaway bed—and roll away it did! After a couple hours of sleep, one of us had all the bedding on one section of the bed, which had moved a couple feet from the other half. Granted it didn't have far to go in our 14-by-7-foot apartment. We shared a bathroom with seven other apartment dwellers. With no cooking stove, we figured that the two electrical outlets and our wedding gift appliances would meet our needs, but each time we plugged in an appliance, fuses blew. Nevertheless it was a happy home."

Kate says, "Even though our rent was $75 a month, we had to share the bath in our first apartment. We rented the front part of an old house, and an elderly woman lived in the back part. Unfortunately, she *died* in that shared bathroom while we were living there!"

Alli says, "I'm beginning to think newlyweds who move into plush first homes miss out on a lot. They won't have any stories like this to tell their children! Claudia, do you remember your first home?"

"Oh yes! It was an upstairs apartment in the home of an elderly couple who had converted spare bedrooms into a small furnished apartment. One pitfall in such an arrangement was the absence of door locks and our landlord's indifference to privacy. When our landlady strolled into our apartment one Saturday afternoon, a love-making session came to an abrupt end!"

"That should teach you to pay your rent on time!" quips Sally.

Garage Apartments

"Our first home was in a garage! People often built apartments above their detached garages. If we forgot to pay our rent on time, our landlady would ring the doorbell at the bottom of the stairs and call in her Yiddish accent, 'Don't you have the money, already?'"

Celia continues, "As Minnesota natives, we didn't have first-hand experience with the ways of other cultures. When our refrigerator shorted out, we asked to put perishable items in our landlady's Kosher refrigerator until ours was fixed. Pork was prohibited, of course, and even the beef had to be wrapped extra well before she would consent to storing that in her fridge."

"Who's next? Barbara?" asks Alli.

"John was in the Navy. When he came home on furlough during the summer of 1957, we were married," says Barbara. "He was stationed in San Diego, so our first home was a block from the ocean. No children were allowed there, so when Jane was born the next year, we moved into the city and lived in a furnished apartment above a garage."

...And Trailer Houses

Marilyn's hand goes up. "Jerome was entering the seminary when we got married in 1957. Housing on campus was for single men only, and many seminary professors were still opposed to students being married. I was teaching in a suburb, and apartments were scarce in the St. Paul/Minneapolis area, so we purchased a 28-foot trailer house. We lived in it throughout our seminary years. It was cozy for two but crowded when we added a baby."

Alli looks to Celia for another kind of story.

Welcome to the Neighborhood

"The Iron Range's economic decline caused a job layoff for engineers in 1961, so we were transferred to Gary (Indiana) one month before our daughter was born. We rented a new house. Our moving van took up most of the driveway while being unloaded, so Gene parked our car across the street. Later that afternoon, we were pleasantly surprised to be welcomed by our neighbor who brought us a homemade cake. Her overture was as much an apology as a welcome. A friend had backed his car out of her driveway right into Gene's newly-painted car across the street. Her friend's name and face seemed familiar. It turned out that he and Gene had lived in the same barracks at Fort Leonard Wood during a three-month tour in the army."

"How appropriate!" Sally adds. "It fulfilled an old army farewell: 'I hope we bump into each other again sometime.'"

Alli prods us for insights into the male psyche that helped us get through those early years—and the ones to come. "Keeping in mind your aggregate marriage experience totals nearly 500 years—half a millennium, I'm listening very carefully to your words of wisdom."

The Male Mind

The Male Mind: *Men Prefer Comfort*

Claudia smiles and begins. "Now, Alli, don't hold your breath waiting for wise words! With 500 years comes a capacity to laugh at ourselves and our husbands. Anyway, a long time ago I read something that said: 'A man will wear anything comfortable no matter how old. A woman will wear anything new no matter how uncomfortable.' I think there's some truth to that—at least the part about men.

"Some thirty years ago, my husband had a red plaid shirt that must have been the most comfortable shirt ever made! It was his favorite, and he wore it much of the time. In those days, it was common to repair favorite garments, even when the repairs were obvious. When his shirt collar wore out, I turned the collar. When the elbows wore out, I cut off the sleeves. Finally, the pockets wore out, so I used material left from the long sleeves and made new pockets. He still wore that old shirt. At last, he gave it up, allowing me to give it to a church rummage sale. A few days later, Martin saw a man downtown wearing his favorite shirt. He tells me that he stopped the gentleman to compliment him on his fine taste in shirts!"

Laughing, Alli asks for more insights into the male psyche. Claudia says she has another slant.

The Male Mind: *Technology Works Best*

"Men and women approach problem solving in different ways. But my example may be as much about differences with the scientific mind as between male and female ways of coping.

"We have a wonderful new home, but we have had some problems with ants. They love to make themselves right at home in our kitchen—under the kitchen sink, in the pantry, in the cupboard drawers, behind the refrigerator and stove, or they march right across a kitchen counter!! One morning when Martin was going to heat his coffee, he found the microwave swarming with ants. I heard him say, 'Look at this!' Racing in, I grabbed a wad of wet paper towels and started wiping up ants. That was not this scientist's approach. 'Wait' he said, and, turning on the oven, he microwaved those ants to a crisp."

The Male Mind: *Me Hunt, You Cook*

"I'm reminded of Jack's pheasant hunting experiences while he was on seminary internship in South Dakota," starts Laura. "His only experience with a gun had been in shooting galleries at Coney Island. When he went pheasant hunting, he fancied himself the frontiersman, bringing home game for his family's table. His hunter's vest was so laden with shells, he could hardly stand upright. The last day of a long season, he finally did bring home a pheasant he'd shot...accidentally. It looked so lonely in the oversized freezer locker he had optimistically rented. By my calculations, this solo bird had cost us about $150! We were both working so hard that year, the cost was worth the diversion of our running joke about Jack's hunting prowess."

"Probably cost what 'pheasant under glass' would sell for at a fancy world-class restaurant!" someone comments, amid the laughter.

The Male Mind: *Give Me Mood Music*

Dana remembers, "For our fourth wedding anniversary, Chris' best pals decided to add some items to our home's decor. They tied bells to the bed, put droopy dried flowers in a vase, and left two of those huge Salvo tablets and two aspirin tablets beside the bed. Two tablets were labeled for self-control and two were for birth-control! When we crawled into bed, it sounded like a concert of bell chimes!"

The Male Mind: *A Risk Factor in Helpmate*

Sally pipes up, "Alli, I'm so glad you are the one operating the recorder! One of my more embarrassing moments happened when I taped Paul's band's performance at a music festival.

"Three judges sat with their backs to the audience to critique and rate each band. I was in the audience with the tape recorder, and the moment Paul raised his arms to give the downbeat, I flicked the switch. Unfortunately, I hit the play button and whatever was already on the tape came blaring out—very loud, very obvious, very embarrassing! With professional cool, the judges refrained from turning around. But, Paul froze in his arms-raised stance. I could almost see his eyes roll to the back of his head as I fumbled with the machine. Finally, I found the right button and recorded the concert. All three judges rated Paul's band 'Excellent.' I was so worried that if they didn't get that rating, I was in deep trouble! Since then, nobody's asked me to operate a recorder for them."

Alli invites more stories.

The Male Mind: *Flying a Grasshopper is Fun*

"Don and I have never had a fight in thirty years, but that is not to say we don't have differences," Elizabeth laughs. "A big one is his love—and my dislike—of flying, especially in small planes! Don was a Navy pilot whose love of flying continues to this day. As a member of a flying club, he has access to a small plane we've used a couple of times to fly to North Dakota. However, my uneasiness in a small plane prevents me from being a frequent flyer.

"At a national air show in Wisconsin, Don met a pilot from Santa Fe who has a couple of Military T-34 trainers, the kind of planes Don learned to fly in the Navy, where he learned aerobatics. He was thrilled to fly the T-34 again. Flying upside down is not my idea of fun, so I went shopping.

"Recently, Don bought an ultra light plane. Because the fuselage is a 23-foot piece of aluminum irrigation pipe, and the covering is lime green dacron sailcloth, I describe it as a grasshopper!

"The attraction of an ultra light is being able to fly low and slow. It takes off and lands at 25 miles per hour. I may never see this 'grasshopper' in the air because I refuse to watch Don fly it."

Alli now looks at Ann to continue the topic of husbands' interests.

The Male Mind: *A Husband At Sea (On His Sailboat)*

"Your husband has an equally unusual leisure time activity, Ann," suggests Alli. "Crossing the ocean in a sailboat?"

"Yes...he finds it challenging."

"How many times has he done this and how long does it take to cross the Atlantic?" asks Alli.

"He has crossed five times, and our children have accompanied him at different times, but I have not. It takes four to six weeks to cross depending on where one starts and ends the voyage."

"Imagine spending four to six weeks seeing water only! The accommodations are obviously very comfortable to be able to spend that much time on the boat. Why haven't you gone along?" questions Alli, showing her interest with a smile.

"It's just not something I need to do to feel fulfilled, and I would feel rather claustrophobic after a few days confined to a sailboat. I'm afraid I would find it more uncomfortable than challenging. However, living as we did for many years in a city on Lake Michigan, as a family we spent several weeks every summer cruising on Lake Michigan, and I have sailed through all the Great Lakes, but crossing the Atlantic is not something I feel compelled to do."

First Ladies of the Parish

Or...I Married a Pastor

Laura and Marilyn are asked about their roles as pastors' wives. "Our first exposure to the parish ministry came in 1957 when Jack interned in South Dakota," begins Laura. "Our salary was $120 a month plus a one-bedroom apartment. Alli, to give you some idea of costs, we bought our first new car—a 1957 Chevrolet station wagon for $2400. Our car payments were $75 a month.

"Because his supervising pastor became acting district president, Jack was often left on his own with more than 3,000 members. He also had the university campus ministry.

"Each Sunday in the summer, a sunrise worship service was held at the local drive-in theatre. One Sunday morning, I placed the speaker on my car window and sang the hymns by myself. Perched high up on a rickety wood platform, Jack conducted the service. When he took out his sermon notes and began...'Dear Friends in Christ...' a gust of wind blew all his notes away, scattering them on the ground far below. 'Let's all sing that last hymn again while the ushers find my sermon,' Jack announced over the P.A. I was relieved to be in the privacy of my car as I started to laugh at this uncomfortable situation that my husband handled so well.

"There were other times when his ministerial actions made me roll my eyes. One Sunday, while kneeling at the altar rail for communion, I watched another gust of wind blow all the communion wafers off his silver plate. Jack calmly collected them from the carpet, reverently placed them on the altar, and got fresh wafers from the sacristy. Judging from the horrified looks on some faces of members from this Polish Catholic neighborhood, I'd guess a few half-expected a bolt of lightning to zap Jack for this 'profane' event. Then there was the time at the end of a very formal service in a large congregation when Jack raised his hand and said 'May the Lord bless you and keep you, may....' He just stopped, unable to remember the rest of the benediction. After what seemed to me an eternity, he made up something that was a miserable excuse for a benediction. We learned that pastors and spouses have to have a sense of humor amidst the seriousness and stresses of ministry."

Alli says, "We get a picture of learning to live life in the parish. How about life in the parsonage?"

Laura continues, "Well, one bizarre experience stands out. In our first parsonage, I noticed that my underwear and some clothes were disappearing. Since we lived in Chicago, I always kept the doors locked. One day, 13-year-old Leo, the son of a leading member of our congregation, came to my back door, made some small talk, and then asked if I would show him what a woman looks like naked. Five months pregnant, I almost lost it! We spoke with his parents and arranged some long-overdue therapy for the boy. But that wasn't the end of it. Apparently Leo had somehow been getting into our house. One day, a confused neighbor came over to show us a brown paper bag filled with undergarments that he found behind some machinery in his garage. Later, another neighbor came waving a bra he'd found hanging on his lawn mower. I never admitted they were mine! I was horrified and repulsed to realize that Leo had secreted my underwear around the neighborhood."

Alli turns to Marilyn. "What parish anecdotes come to mind for you, Marilyn?"

"Jerome's internship assignment in Montana was at a two-point parish plus a preaching point shared by several other Protestant pastors. When we arrived, we learned that Jerome's supervising pastor had had a heart attack shortly before; so he cut back on outpost activities. Jerome's first assignment was to conduct the funeral service of an old miner. A new pastor dreads that first funeral, but Jerome wasn't even a pastor yet! He had the service in the mortuary, and only two people came. The old miner was buried in his World War I army uniform.

"Jerome took his turn conducting services. Women of the altar guild would set up for communion before the service. When it was a Methodist service, they served grape juice. When the Lutherans were there, wine was served. One Sunday they mixed Methodist grape juice and Lutheran wine together! We suspect the supply of wine was nearly depleted. Communion wine was not sold in grocery stores; we had to send away for it.

"In love with Montana, we were delighted when Jerome received his first call to the heart of wheat country. We sent our large items ahead on an empty cattle truck headed west to pick up cattle. Our arrival in July coincided with harvest, when all other activity comes to a halt. Consequently, the parsonage wasn't ready for us. It was a mess; even the windows were painted shut. Nonetheless, we quickly came to love those dear people. A foul-up in communication, complicated by harvest time, was responsible for their unprepared welcome.

"I recall one Sunday morning when a bat got into the sanctuary. During Jerome's sermon, this bat began swooping down on the congregation. People were dodging its flying, furry body. Jerome lost their attention. So, he stopped the sermon until the ushers finally trapped the bat."

Alli is feeling something of a generation or culture gap, but she's laughing at these light-hearted recollections. "It's fun to hear about your experiences. You've shown me the importance of having a sense of humor as you live life intimately with another person. On my private list of 'Requirements for a Marriage Partner,' I'm going to elevate a sense of humor to a much higher position.

"After a break, we're going to talk about the religious base for marriage and some other serious aspects of life together."

3

Christian Marriage: God's One New Person

There Will be Times

There will be times
    when your patience runs out
    when the children just pout,
    when you wish they were older
    or wish they were younger.

There will be days
    when the rain just won't stop,
    when your cake is a flop,
    when the house seems too small,
    when your friends just don't call.

There will always be
    complaints to repeat
    feelings of defeat
    periods of depression,
    feelings of aggression.

But there will come a time
*   when you'll have regrets*
*   that you took backward steps*
*   from your wedded bliss*
*   and marriage happiness.*

For years pass so quickly—
*   your daughter gets married,*
*   your son goes to college,*
*   the gray hair takes over,*
*   your husband—a rover?*

Don't neglect during motherhood years
*   to keep husband content*
*   on your marriage be bent.*
*   Make him want to come home*
*   —so you'll not be alone.*

Give him your love
*   and all your affection.*
*   When he looks in a mirror,*
*   contentment...his reflection.*

—Lois Qualben

A Serious Side of Marriage

Alli shifts our attention. "Blue Garter Club members represent nearly 500 years of marriage—anywhere from 29 to 36 years each. How do you account for that?" Alli asks the question in a general way, smiling, waiting for a possible silly response. Quick-witted Sally doesn't disappoint her. "The house was surrounded by a moat. He hid my shoes. When he didn't have me handcuffed to the kitchen sink, there was this ball and chain." As though an afterthought, she added, "Oh yes...and his after-shave triggered a severe hypnotic reflex that forced me to constantly repeat, "Yes, Dear. Whatever you say, Dear."

Alli grins, "Okay...Any other insights, anyone, or shall we move on?"

Celia says, "Gene and I were 24 years old, mature, educated, and had satisfying careers. We had similar social, educational, and most important, spiritual backgrounds. These ingredients all help to account for our lasting marriage."

Alli extends Celia's thoughts, "Would it be fair to add that you were old enough to know what you wanted, and you were ready for marriage?"

"Right. And, because we had a baby nine months later, we also had to be ready for parenthood. That first year of marriage brought lots of changes for each of us."

"Diaper changes?" Sally again.

"That, too!" laughs Celia.

Audrey addresses Alli. "None of us ventured far from our families' values in finding our spouses. Your generation, Alli, is so different. The job market takes your contemporaries all over the country where they meet people with entirely different perspectives on family life, morals, religion, nationality. Sometimes these marriages work, but too many of them don't. I do think similar backgrounds is a big factor."

"Complete acceptance of the other person is also important," says Elizabeth. "Don and I have never tried to change each other. Knowing each other's faults, but accepting them as part of our whole person, has helped us get along so well. Not many wives can say that their husband has never said a cross word to them in thirty years. I can—because Don is so easy going. We may have wanted to clobber each other at times, but we have never had a fight."

"How do you work out your differences then?" asks Alli.

"Except for the flying matter, our priorities are so similar that we don't seem to have any notable differences," answers Elizabeth.

Aimee nods her head, as though in agreement with Elizabeth. "That description fits my husband, too. We are both very laid back; not very adventuresome, perhaps evidenced by having stayed in one location most of our married life."

Advice to Newlyweds

Alli presses further. "I have an idea that it's more than just accepting your mates that has helped your marriages last so long."

Laura responds, "Sheer will, a lot of hard work, flexibility, prayer, forgiveness, trust, and..."

"And, togetherness! Don't go your separate ways!" interrupts Sarah. "Our marriage almost ended after about ten years because we began to drift apart. When I realized we were living almost separate lives and that our marriage was falling apart, I sought counseling. We were able to once again build a strong relationship. But I must say that the counseling I received through our church wasn't very helpful to me. Our deep commitment to our marriage, in spite of everything, was probably what saved it. Seeing our marriage almost fail was a turning point in my life. The advice I'd give newlyweds is to communicate with each other—for the sake of your marriage, to express appreciation for each other, respect each other, pray together, and forgive each other."

A Non-traditional Marriage

Alli continues. "I find it interesting that you mentioned 'staying together and not going separate ways' because Ann and Charles have maintained a long marriage while living apart much of the time. Can you tell us how that has worked, Ann?"

"Charles and I have had a non-traditional marriage for several years, which has allowed each of us to pursue our individual interests and to live our lives to the fullest. We have maintained a relationship and a family environment for our children. And we have preserved the home they grew up in for them to come back to as adults."

"How did you happen to begin this long-distance marriage?" asks Alli.

"Charles was offered a position in Washington, D.C. with the U.S. Department of State. At the time, I had just been elected to the City Council after a vigorous campaign; our youngest son, Kon, was still in high school and the other two children were at St. Olaf College. I did not want to uproot myself, nor did I think it would be good to uproot Kon and move him to a different environment at this point in his life. On the other hand, it was a good opportunity for Charles. The decision we reached was not easy, but has been a good experience for both of us. Charles moved to Washington, while Kon and I stayed in Wisconsin. Needless to say, it was 'revolutionary' in that city and at that time. Now, of course, commuter marriages are more common and accepted as a way of life for many couples who wish to pursue different careers."

"And you continued the long-distance marriage even after your children were out of the nest," comments Laura.

"Yes. My City Council work was important to me, and I served eight years in that capacity. When I moved to Washington four years ago, I found an interesting job, as well as opportunities for acting in both film and

videos, which I didn't have in Wisconsin. So I am enjoying my life here. Charles has now retired, however, and
moved back to our home in Wisconsin, so we are still
fulfilling our own individual needs."

Alli summarizes, "Thanks, Ann. Your marriage is
certainly not traditional, but you have shown us some
benefits of being non-traditional."

When Your Husband's Lover Is Another Man

"With only one divorce among you, the Blue Garter
Club is quite unusual," Alli observes. "And Elizabeth's
second marriage has been blessed for thirty years, so she
ranks with the rest of you in longevity of marriage. We
know your first husband, Lionel, was a homosexual,
Elizabeth. We know it was traumatic for you, so we
appreciate your willingness to talk about it. Are you
ready for this?"

"Yes, but I need to forewarn you that very little
remains in my memory from those two years. What
confusion I went through! After this baffling, devastating experience, eventually I faced what happened—
squarely and realistically. I faced the hurts. Then, very
deliberately I let go of it all—handed it over to God—
and moved on with my life. In a very real sense, God has
separated those two years from me as far as east is from
the west.

"I'm sure you are wondering why Lionel ever got
married. I think in his case, as with others, it was a
matter of covering up. Remember, we're talking the
mid-fifties, when homosexual activity was neither out
in the open nor understood. I suspect another reason
Lionel wanted to marry me was because he hoped to
start his own business, and he knew I could finance it for
him."

Claudia notes, "Several of us took part in your beautiful wedding. As you two drove away in Lionel's convertible, you were a picture of happiness. Settling into a Minneapolis apartment seemed glamorous to me."

Elizabeth ignores Claudia's compliment and says, "You know, it took me a while to figure out that our marriage wasn't the norm. I'd have to say that back then most of us were very naive about homosexuality. We may have talked about it once or twice in the dorm, but that was it. After we'd been married a few months, Lionel began pointing out people and saying things like, 'That person is gay. I can tell by looking at him.' He did this so many times, it became a fetish. I couldn't figure out why he was so adamant about calling my attention to homosexuals. This was my first clue, although it took more than a year before I suspected *he* was gay. And, it took another year to decide to get a divorce. My minister told me that I could likely get an annulment, but a divorce was quicker. There were no divorces among my 39 first cousins. Would I be the first? Making the decision for divorce wasn't easy for me, even under those circumstances."

"You just used the term 'gay,' a term which wasn't used at that time. He probably used the word homosexual or maybe 'queer'?" asks Audrey.

"Yes. I suppose so. I don't even remember what his terminology was," Elizabeth continues.

"Lionel was teaching science in a private school that specialized in training medical laboratory technicians. His friend, Will, needed a place to live for awhile—for economic reasons, I was told. We had a spare room, so why not help out a friend in need? I was agreeable. Busy with my own teaching career, I was gone a lot, so having someone else living with us didn't bother me that much. Will lived with us for about a year. It took a long time before I suspected something was going on between the two of them in my absence. Maybe it took me a long time to become suspicious because of my naivete' and because it didn't seem possible. Certain looks were exchanged between them, certain words were spoken. My day started early as I drove a long ways to school, so going to bed early was important. The two men often stayed up late to supposedly talk about the business Lionel wanted to start!"

"Ohhh Boy!" Audrey mutters.

"You're probably wondering whether or not we had a 'normal' sex life. Looking back, I guess not, but at the time, I didn't know any better; so I thought it was normal enough. In our marriage, lovemaking was hardly the frequent activity people assume about newlyweds."

"Did you ever argue or confront him about his behavior or about his friend moving into your home?" asks Kate.

"No. As I said before, I have let go of what happened then, so I can't really remember a lot after 32 years. We got along okay, kind of an awkward truce. But, if there was any kind of disagreement or problem, he always blamed me. Any suspicions I had about him, I kept to myself."

"Elizabeth, I remember you telling me how horrified you were to find your lingerie in Will's dresser drawer," Laura comments.

"Did that happen, too? I don't remember it. Never once did we talk about Lionel's relationship with Will, or that he was homosexual, or anything having to do with that life style. Everything was 'hunky-dory' as far as he was concerned. He claimed our marriage was just fine."

"Big time denial goes a long way, doesn't it?" says Barbara.

Elizabeth continues. "We didn't ever discuss divorce. My excuse for going home to North Dakota was to help my sister-in-law who was having a baby. School was out for the summer, so I packed some things I considered valuable and left Minneapolis. My brother, Cliff, was the first person to hear of my divorce plans and the reason. Cliff's reaction was, 'I always thought there was something strange about him.' Together, we told my mother. But first, it was necessary to explain to her what the term homosexual meant. Her reaction was typical for a small town mother in 1960: 'What are the neighbors going to say?'"

"Elizabeth, you and I had lunch together that summer when we were visiting Martin's parents in Fargo," Claudia remembers. "You told me on the phone you had seen your doctor, and I assumed you were pregnant. Then you said you were filing for divorce. It wasn't until we were together at lunch that you told me the reason; I was shocked. First of all, divorce wasn't common in our circles. Plus, homosexuality was almost unheard of. It was hard to imagine that someone we all knew throughout our college years was a homosexual."

"We had lunch?" Elizabeth looks confused. "I don't remember that either! I filed for divorce; the divorce papers were served; he didn't contest it. The divorce was granted after the required length of time. My attorney arranged for me to go back to our apartment to remove my belongings on a Saturday when Lionel was gone. After I got the divorce and mentioned my reason, several people told me they suspected he was gay and wondered why he ever got married."

"What were the 'formal' grounds for your divorce?" asks Alli.

"My attorney conferred with the judge in advance; they decided that my divorce would be granted on the grounds that Lionel didn't attend school functions with me, and so I had to drive by myself at night to attend PTA meetings. The court proceeding took all of four minutes. Renae and another teacher friend told the judge that, basically, I was alone all the time. Handling the grounds for divorce this way meant there would be no scandal from court records mentioning that Lionel was homosexual."

"That you have cut off so much of it from your memory is indicative of the trauma you went through," says Alli as she writes a note to herself. "I'm reminding myself to return to how you women have dealt with your own hurtful memories. Deliberate letting-go is one way that's helped Elizabeth. But let's come back to this later, shall we?" Thoughtful expressions are on 14 faces in the room.

"Elizabeth, we are so thankful you built a new life, married Don, and have enjoyed a blessed home life ever since," Alli concludes.

Christian Marriage: God's One New Person

Alli says, " I want to mention the husband descriptions you prepared prior to this meeting. Some of the adjectives you used to describe your husbands were exactly the words I expected to see: loving, faithful, loyal, dependable, thoughtful, supportive, forgiving, generous, intelligent, interesting. But what surprised me was also seeing words such as: dull, boring, stuffy, predictable. The contrast between courtship qualities and how you describe your long-time husbands is both funny and interesting. In your marriages, you have definitely 'settled in.' I recall reading about this in *Mere Christianity* by C.S. Lewis:

> "'Now no feeling can be relied on to last in its full intensity, even to last at all….And, in fact, whatever people say, the state called 'being in love' usually does not last. If the old fairy-tale ending 'They lived happily ever after' is taken to mean 'They felt for the next fifty

years exactly as they felt the day before they were married,' then it says what probably never was nor ever could be true, and would be highly undesirable if it were. Who could bear to live in that excitement for even five years?'

"'But, of course, ceasing to be 'in love' does not mean ceasing to love. Love in this second sense—love as distinct from "being in love" is not merely a feeling. It is a deep unity, maintained by the will and deliberately strengthened by habit; reinforced by (in Christian marriages) the grace which both [partners] ask and receive from God."

Alli continues, "He goes on to explain how you can maintain this love even in those moments when you don't *like* your spouse, because that happens in the same way that you love yourself even when you don't like yourself! And he talks about 'being in love' as that state of being that moves a couple to make promises of fidelity, but the quieter love enables the couple to keep that promise. Permit me to read one more sentence where he compares marital love to a running engine. 'It is on this love [i.e. the quieter love] that the engine of marriage is run; being in love was the explosion that started it.'"

"The Blue Garter Club has nearly five hundred years of that 'quiet love' commitment!" Alli turns now to Laura and, while referring to her notes, says, "I'd like to hear more about the One New Person created by God for Christian marriage. You have published Bible studies on this topic, Laura. Please elaborate."

Laura responds, "We all agree that successful marriages are not easy to achieve. Most people marry with the idea of living happily ever after; but they'd better be prepared to work hard to achieve that happiness. In addition to comments already made, I think it's important to enjoy each other's company. Ann has already shown us that living apart and drifting apart are not the same thing. Meaningful for Jack and me has been the Biblical teaching that God brings two individuals together in marriage to become something bigger than both of us—a God-created One New Person that Paul described in Ephesians."

Laura explains, "Christian marriage is the epitome of a unique kind of oneness in human relationships. The original theme of 'two shall become one flesh' as referenced in Genesis 2:24 creates a whole new being that exceeds the sum of two singles. Think of it as God bringing two dimes together and creating a quarter. It is so much more than a 'partnership' or merger between husband and wife. At the altar on our wedding day, a unique new being is created by God. This is what my husband and I try to stress in our Bible study materials."

"Thanks, Laura." Alli continues, "C.S. Lewis has something to say about that in *Mere Christianity*, too:

> "The Christian idea of marriage is based on Christ's words that a man and wife are to be regarded as a single organism—for that is what the words 'one flesh' would be in modern English.... The inventor of the human machine was telling us that its two halves, the male and the female, were made to be combined together in pairs, not simply on the sexual level, but totally combined. The monstrosity of sexual intercourse outside marriage is that those who indulge in it are trying to isolate one kind of union (the sexual) from all the other kinds of union which were intended to go along with it and make up the total union."

"He uses several analogies to describe the two sexes combining into one flesh in marriage, comparing them to a lock and key as being one mechanism, a violin and bow as being one musical instrument; each needs the other to be completely functional."

Audrey raises her hand. "I saw an anonymous quotation recently that said: 'What's so remarkable about love at first sight? It's when people have been looking at each other for years that it becomes remarkable.' Through long marriages, we come to realize that experiencing life together is truly a gift. Over a span of years, we accept each other, adjust to each other, and truly understand each other. Because we build a foundation and a history together, it's possible to reap the joy and blessings of contentment in your relationship as husband and wife as the years go by."

Alli thanks Audrey and concludes with, "On the surface, your marriages seem to be the kind God intended."

Letting Go of the Hurts

"Earlier I made a note to myself to draw you out with regard to dealing with hurtful memories. Naming and letting go of a hurt was one way for Elizabeth to survive her trauma and heartache of marriage to a homosexual. What insights do you have?" asks Alli.

"Severe trauma remaining from childhood should be sorted out by a professional. In the '50s, counseling wasn't as readily available as it is today," suggests Kate.

"I talked to both my pastor and my doctor," says Elizabeth, "and their counseling was helpful to me in making my decision to file for divorce. But I had to deal with the hurtful memories of those two years in my own way—by blocking it off from the rest of my life, so those hurts could not poison the years that followed."

Alli asks, "How do others deal with hurtful memories within a marriage?"

"Don't let your hurts become memories. Talk!" suggests Laura. "When you openly talk about hurtful words or actions, it's easier to forgive and easier to forget—and let go of it. Avoid keeping a record of wrongs for later reference. When we hang on to our hurts, they become cumbersome burdens, sapping us of energy better used on more positive aspects of living. Clear the air. Then start anew. This becomes a very practiced reliance on Jesus, whose name is Alpha-Omega—the beginning and the end. Face the hurt, then hand it over to our Lord."

"The Bible tells us not to let the sun set on our wrath," offers Dana, "lest the devil gain a foothold to drive a wedge between us."

Alli is taking these comments to heart. With a thoughtful expression, she says, "You are acutely aware how difficult it is to live intimately with another person for many decades. You have said that sometimes the joys and blessings barely cover the hurts and anger. But your compassion and acceptance have become apparent in your discussions. Why don't we take a break before we start talking about our families?"

Dana interrupts. "I'd like to share a poem I recently wrote in response to my daughter's request that I contribute something original for the back of her marriage bulletin. I've set this to music, but since I didn't happen to bring along my pipe organ or my harmonica or my bag pipes, I'd be honored if you'd let me read my heartfelt wish for my daughter and her new husband."

Together May You Ever Be

Today tomorrow and always
*   together may you ever be*
with God's strong arm around you
*   content with life and free.*
Free to love each other
*   as He first loved you*
free to be your own being
*   pleasing Him in all you do.*

Today tomorrow and always
*   together may you ever be*
striving to improve this earthly time
*   this time to which you hold the key.*
The key to choose the way you live
*   your goals, and yes, your closest friends.*
The key to every unknown pathway
*   with God to guide you to the end.*

Today tomorrow and always
*   together may you ever be*
forever in God's favor
*   with the blessings of His peace.*
Blessings of His tender love
*   so gentle and so kind*
Blessings of His precious grace
*   His Holy Spirit divine.*

Today tomorrow and always
*   together may you ever be*
filled with love overflowing
*   in your hearts for all to see*
this love you both are willing
*   now with each other to share*
God's love will bind and keep you together
Today, tomorrow and always—
Always, tomorrow and today.

© Dee Hoff Larson

4

And Baby Makes Three or Four...or More

Welcome, Dear Babe

Welcome, dear babe, into this world
A whole new life has been unfurled.
Your father and I are without a doubt
the most proud and grateful parents about.

Thinking back to that day you arrived,
'tis a miracle your father ever survived.
If you've seen a grown man fall apart,
you know it's enough to break one's heart.

Poor Daddy was shaking like a leaf
as he peered through the window in awe and relief,
for a hospital nursery is a frightening place,
when a Dad sees his newborn face to face.

Papa was almost bursting his buttons
as he loudly proclaimed,
"That's my little cuttons."
"See everyone—that pink one there—
the one with the nose and the ears and the hair."

"Time's up" said the nurse as he wheeled baby away;
*   Daddy began to protest and to bray—*
"Don't take her away cuz I'm sure you did see
*   that my baby just started to recognize me."*

At that I gave up and led the poor man
*   back down the corridor by the hand*
I tucked the box of cigars 'neath his arm
*   and prayed God to keep him safe from all harm.*

Dad wasn't the only one that day
*   to beam, to cackle, to coo, and to sway;*
for I was as proud and thankful as he
*   that God bestowed Motherhood's hand on me.*

We hope that your brother and sister will be
*   as elated and full of cheer as we.*
I s'pose you think you'll take over the house;
*   give us time—we'll adjust to a new boss.*

We welcome you, baby, to our family;
*   you must know you're received happily.*
We thank you Lord Jesus Christ above
*   for this priceless gift of child love.*

— Lois Qualben

* * *

Alli had asked us to submit stories from our own experiences that could be used in various places in the book. She now looks around the room, smiling. Then with a furrowed brow and lowered voice, she begins reading from a prepared manuscript.

"Oh, don't look at her! You've seen her before! Look at this!" The doctor's voice was strong and reassuring as he gestured toward the tiny baby in the bassinet. "It's a boy!"

I was being wheeled from the delivery room to a room across the hall. The waiting room was nearby and the doctor could see my husband sitting there, now looking toward the noise in the hallway. The doctor motioned him over, and he came to my bedside. He took my hands and asked, "Are you all right?"

The anesthetic was still affecting me; I seemed to be drifting in and out, but I distinctly heard my husband's question and the doctor's amusing response. A short time earlier, the doctor had provided me with the same information, and I had proudly announced, "I knew it would be a boy!" It was shortly after midnight, Halloween Day, 1959.

My prayers were answered. Thank you, God, for a strong and healthy baby.

* * *

"Blue Garter Club members certainly did comply with the motherhood expectations of women of the 1950s. I just counted the total number of children from your group, and you women have mothered 45 children. Since my mother was also a member of your group, I could include my brother and myself for a total of 47. Family sizes range from two to six. What a prolific group!"

Alli introduces the topic and keeps the dialogue moving on course. Starting the recorder, she comments on how relaxed the group has become, even with the tape running. Her standard instructions to "keep talking" seem superfluous; women don't usually need such reminding!

Biological Babies

"I like this new baby story. It reminds me of when Kevin was born. I was also drifting in and out from the anesthetic, but I heard the nurse in the delivery room speaking Norwegian. It struck me so funny because I was thinking that this new baby of ours is full-blooded Norwegian, and the nurse is speaking to him in his native tongue." Dana is recalling her first delivery room experience.

"Obviously that hospital was in Minnesota, the Norwegian-speaking capital of the U.S.," volunteers Audrey.

"You must have thought you had died and gone to Norway!" quips Sally.

Celia comments, "Our babies were born before fathers were allowed in the delivery room. I'm sure our husbands can remember sitting in the waiting room until the doctor emerged with the big announcement. Our two babies were born in hospitals that restricted visitors to husbands and clergy. I can also relate to what you were saying about the anesthetic. In those days, women giving birth were usually given an anesthetic; I wasn't aware of any natural childbirth classes. There certainly has been a lot of progress in obstetrics. I'm the mother of an obstetrician, and, as you all know, that obstetrician is female!" Celia smiles proudly.

Renae laughs, "At least your husbands were nearby. Even though the hospital was only a five-minute walk from where Jerry worked, his military superior kept my husband at work so he missed the birth of his first son. And he missed the second one, too, because I flew to a special military hospital for that birth. The third time, he was drinking coffee in the hospital cafeteria, after being sent there by the delivery room nurses!"

"You are not alone, Renae. When our third child was ready to be born, I went to the hospital by myself, in a taxi, at midnight," says Ann. "Charles stayed home with the other children because we didn't want to disturb anyone at midnight. You see, I had already been in the hospital for four days because of a nosebleed that wouldn't stop. Then I went home for several hours and returned at midnight. It was no big deal!"

Barbara raises her hand. "When our first daughter was born, the umbilical cord was wrapped around her neck, and she was blue. As a 'blue baby,' she had to go through a lot of testing to make sure her heart was okay. I had so many stitches, I couldn't even sit; so on the way home from the hospital, I had to lie down in the back seat of the car and watch the tree tops whiz by."

Laura adds, "We lived in Chicago when our first child was born. My obstetricians were fine doctors but, in the 1960s, these particular doctors were 'brutal' when it came to weight gain. If I gained an extra pound, I'd cancel my appointment rather than face their disapproval. Although I had gained only eight pounds throughout my pregnancy, one month I had added a couple of extra pounds. While I was on the examining table, my doctor countered with, 'Where is the Armour Star label?'"

"Laura, I remember you telling us about that in your Round Robin letter. Since you were so slender to begin with, I wondered why all the fuss about gaining weight," Claudia says with a quizzical expression.

"In spite of premature arrivals and my minimal weight gain, one of our babies weighed over nine pounds. If I'd gained more weight, delivery would've been more difficult" Laura responds. "Being pregnant with my first child was most unpleasant. I remember waiting for the bus each day. I clutched the light post as the wind whipped off Lake Michigan, biting my legs and freezing the tears on my face. I wore my 3-inch Nixon button while all the other riders on the bus wore Kennedy buttons. This was southside Chicago, 1960! Each time the bus stopped, I debated if I should get off because I was going to be sick. Falling asleep on the way to work and missing my stop was a common occurrence.

"Eight months pregnant, I continued to work on the 19th floor of a skyscraper in the Loop. Being 5 foot 2 inches and 'great with child,' I was amused at men's anxious looks when I'd step into the elevator. They'd glance around nervously to see if there might be some-one else in the elevator who would take responsibility if this woman went into labor and, in fact, decided to have the baby before she got to the 19th floor."

Miscarriage: A Lonely Experience

Alli suggests a slight change of direction here. "Perhaps this is a good time to discuss the topic of miscarriage. Laura, please share some of your thoughts about the two miscarriages you suffered."

"I had a miscarriage between the birth of my first and second child, and again between my second and third. It's difficult to empathize if you haven't endured that hurtful experience. The first miscarriage occurred after four months of being terribly ill—I began hemorrhaging. We raced to the hospital, where I was instructed to go to the Emergency Room. I refused and demanded to see my doctor immediately. As we were arguing with hospital personnel, the elevator opened and my doctor appeared. At that moment, he wore angel's wings! He took one look at me and hustled me up to the proper floor. The nurses ignored me, claiming there was no bed. I heard my doctor snap at them, 'Get her one now. Do you want another one to die out here in the corridor?' So began an ordeal.

"I whimpered as the doctor hunted for the veins in my arm. I was shocked when he growled back at me, 'You think *I'm* enjoying this?' Dr. Personality then rushed me into surgery."

"Was this the same doctor who tried to starve you during your first pregnancy?" Elizabeth asks somewhat sarcastically.

Laura smiles and nods. "While vomiting in the recovery room after surgery, I looked up to see the hospital chaplain, a friend of mine. My reaction was to angrily ask, 'What are *you* doing here?' One's manners do tend to go awry under certain conditions, but in retrospect I think he lacked sensitivity regarding my need for privacy. I mean, let me throw up in peace, man! I wasn't back in my room very long before there was a huge crash, and glass flew through my room. A floor was being added to the hospital, and a large plank from that job flew through my window. Now—this is a fine church hospital, but do you think I wasn't eager to get home?

"After a miscarriage, there is a terrible sense of loss. Plans were being made; morning sickness was a way of life—and then comes that pain of a miscarriage. Home from the hospital, my empty arms ached. The body is traumatized from this unnatural happening, and it isn't unusual to suffer depression and exhaustion. I felt tired for several months.

"It's a very lonely time, and it's important for friends and the church to minister to a family in this crisis. The doctor's words of 'It is nature's way of...' are *not* particularly comforting at this time.

"And for women who have infertility problems, a miscarriage must be devastating. Emotions run amok with grief, anger, blame, and even guilt. 'What did I do to deserve this?' is a common question. During the next pregnancy, I was terrified the whole nine months that I would start spotting or hemorrhaging again."

"Thanks, Laura. I think people sometimes trivialize what's gone on before." Alli waits a moment, then directs the discussion once again. "Since I've never been pregnant, I'd never thought much about miscarriages. But obviously, we do need to be more sensitive to women—actually families—in this situation."

Adopted Children

Sarah asks, "How many adopted children do we have in this group?"

Alli looks for those figures and answers, "Five. Okay, are you ready to shift to the topic of adopted children? Laura just mentioned how devastating a miscarriage is for a woman with infertility problems. A lot of advances have been made in treating infertility; but when you were having your children, such treatment wasn't an option. If a woman couldn't get pregnant, she either went through life childless or else the couple adopted. In your group, every one of you who adopted a child also had your own biological children. Adopting was not necessarily done because you didn't think you could bear a child. Is that right?"

A Gift Freely Given

"Well, it's true the three of us who adopted also had our own biological children, but in my case the adopted children came first. We adopted because we thought I couldn't get pregnant," Audrey comments.

Alli invites this talkative, friendly blonde to share her adoption story, and Audrey begins.

"In my Bible studies, I've been amazed to discover how often circumstances of Biblical characters have been similar to my own life. How I identified with the longing of Hannah for a child as she went to the temple and pleaded with the Lord for an opportunity to be a mother! Read the account in I Samuel 1. We had been married three or four years when we felt ready to start a family. My prayers always included a wish to become pregnant and, indeed, it was a pleading from my heart! Nothing happened, so we consulted a doctor. We went through the necessary testing only to be told that if we wanted a child at this time, we should consider adoption.

"After much prayer and deliberation, we contacted Lutheran Social Services of Minneapolis and began proceedings for adoption. In 1962, we received a call from the agency informing us that a nine-month-old baby boy was available! What a quandary I was in! I had prepared for a newborn, and my first thought was, 'What does a nine-month-old baby eat? What are his characteristics? Do we have the right size clothing?'

"Well, needless to say, these thoughts were momentary. We responded that we'd be happy to take this child who was now available!"

"Audrey, you and Art brought your new baby to a reunion of the Blue Garter Club soon after you adopted him, so we got to see him right away," interrupts Kate with a smile.

Audrey acknowledges Kate and then continues. "When I've been asked to share the most joyful experience of my life, my response has always been, 'The receiving of our children through adoption.' Words fail to express the wonder of being handed a child whom we've had no part in conceiving or bringing into this world. We received each child as a gift, freely given! Truly, it is an awesome experience! Our hearts are so filled with humility and thanks to God for His benevolence in bringing about this wonderful event in response to our longings and prayers.

"A familiar verse to many adopted families is this:

> *Not flesh of my flesh*
> *Nor bone of my bone*
> *But still miraculously my own.*
> *Never forget for a single minute*
> *You didn't grow under my heart—*
> *But in it!*

"Yes, indeed, our 'chosen' children are children of our hearts and recipients of our love. Our second son was adopted in 1964, and his adoption was no less a joyous occasion than our first adoption. Then in 1965, I gave birth to a baby girl. She, too, was a special child; she was completely unexpected and provided us with the opportunity to have a family comprised of both sexes. Suddenly our family consisted of three children under the age of four; we no longer needed to plead for more!"

"That happens so often, doesn't it, that a woman gets pregnant after adopting children," Alli comments. "I'm glad you made the comparison to Hannah. It's interesting to realize that a 20th-century woman can have the same feelings as a woman of the Bible. Let's hear another adoption story. Kate?" Alli tries to size up this lady who she'd thought of as Mother Earth. Alli wonders if her first impression is correct.

Adopted Children Join Our Biological Children

Kate begins. "We are parents of four biological children and two adopted children. We had three daughters, and I yearned to have a son. The year was 1967; we were living in South Dakota. At that time, there were so many babies available for adoption that ads were run in the newspapers asking people to adopt newborn babies. When I tell that to people today, they can't believe it; now the ads are from the couples who want so desperately to adopt. Anyway, we also adopted through Lutheran Social Services. During the social worker's visits to our home, he noticed all the pictures on our walls, paintings done by my mother and by me. This turned out to be one of the determining factors in choosing which baby would come to our home.

"Since there were so many babies available, the social workers would sit around a table looking at the files and make comments such as they did with Sterling: 'This baby's mother is an artist, and Kate paints pictures. So, if this baby has any artistic talents, those talents would certainly be encouraged in this home.'

"That is how they chose Sterling for us. It was so exciting, and it turned out that this child *does* have enormous artistic talents.

"When we adopted Sterling, the social worker reported that times were changing with regard to unwed mothers who had been giving up their babies for adoption. Until then, many young women retreated to a home for unwed mothers, secretly gave birth to their babies, and returned home again. Now, she said, these pregnant women had friends come to visit them. The stigma of having a child out of wedlock was waning.

"Two years later, we wanted to adopt another baby boy, so again we contacted Lutheran Social Services. There were still babies available. Our second adopted son was delivered to us by the social worker in an airplane! Our children don't believe the stork brings babies! No, babies come by airplanes! The whole family went out to the airport to pick up our new baby."

Alli is distracted as Kate concludes her story. She realizes she had sold Kate short, as she is not only a mother, but an artist and much more. "It is so interesting to hear these stories. Times have really changed. Thanks, Kate."

Alli nods toward Marilyn, a seemingly self-sufficient and confident woman with graying hair, glasses, and a matter-of-fact manner. "You have an adoption story with a different twist because you adopted a child of a different race."

Adoption of a Multi-Race Child

"Our son, Jeffrey, is a mixture of Native American, Hispanic, and black American, and he is also learning disabled. We adopted Jeff through Lutheran Social Services in 1973, after a two year wait. As Kate mentioned, babies were plentiful in the late 1960s, but this was changing with women keeping their babies and abortion becoming legal. We got caught in that change.

"Since my third pregnancy had been difficult, we decided on adoption. We kept this news a secret until we actually had the baby; only our immediate family knew about it. Our one stipulation on the adoption application was to get a boy. Race was not an issue with us.

"Our new son came to us in a round-about way, and we feel the Holy Spirit led us to Jeff. The Lutheran Social Services social worker in Montana received a call from the state of Wyoming reporting there was a baby boy available there, a mixed-race child. This six-week-old baby was in a children's home; he was considered hard to place. Whenever a hard-to-place child is available, the state agencies contact a church social services agency to help with placement. Our name had come up before this when another child was born but, because that child was a girl, we were never contacted. However, the secretary at the state agency remembered our application papers. This prompted a call to our social worker in Montana. Would we consider adopting this mixed-race baby? They sent a picture. We said absolutely we would take him.

"The five of us traveled to Wyoming to pick up our new baby, who was 2-1/2 months old by now. During the trip, I became terribly sick—nauseated and weak. Jerome had to stop the car so I could lie down on the seat. Everyone else in the family seemed perfectly calm. I was a nervous wreck! We certainly had approached this new episode in our lives with prayer, but the reality of what we were doing suddenly struck like a rush: We were adding to our family a baby who was of a different culture. Not just one different culture, but three. How were we going to handle this? Were we crazy? Would we be able to provide for this child adequately so he would know his roots? Of course, at that time we were unaware of his learning disability."

"How old were your other children when you got Jeff?" asks Alli.

"Our girls were 15 and 11; our son was 8. We didn't really want such an age spread between our 8-year-old son and his new brother but, as I mentioned, there were fewer babies available by the time we got Jeff. Since we already had three natural children, it took longer."

"You mentioned a children's home. He wasn't in a foster home?" Alli questions.

"No, he was in a children's home where there were seven other babies. When we arrived, the nurse placed this baby in my arms; the emotion I felt was beyond description." Marilyn's voice cracks as she pauses momentarily to regain her composure. "His birth parents were teenagers who had relinquished him immediately, and he was placed in the children's home. The administrator told us that they can only give custodial care to these babies and that our new baby really needed a family. Naturally. Little did we know what that meant.

"Equipped with camping gear for the trip, a bassinet, and baby supplies, we headed for a camp site on our trip back to Montana. We wanted to make sure the new baby didn't disturb the other campers with his crying, so we were well prepared for all his needs. Well, he didn't cry. He didn't cry all night long; he didn't cry all day long. He simply didn't react at all. Even the children noticed how unusual it was for a two-month-old baby to be so quiet.

"After a few days at home with us, he began to respond. Then it didn't take long before he reacted to the attention, to the love being poured out to him. He smiled, cooed, laughed, and cried."

"How do you account for his unresponsiveness?" asks Elizabeth.

"In time, the words of the children's home administrator became clear to me. The caregivers did the best they could in giving custodial care, but a baby usually had to be fed on a schedule, not demand. Babies had to wait to receive attention and cuddling. An institutional schedule does not operate on an individual baby's time table, so babies don't necessarily learn that crying brings a response. You all know that babies instinctively cry to announce their needs. Jeff's needs were not often met by crying, so he didn't cry. Since the babies didn't have the same caregiver, they didn't recognize a familiar voice. After a few days in our home, hearing the same voices, seeing the same faces, he really responded."

"How did people in your church and in your community react to the mixed-race issue or to a white family adopting a black child?" asks Alli.

"Bringing a black child home to Missoula really wasn't a problem. Most people in our church were very accepting. For years Missoula had been given a liberal label with the University influence, and this spilled over into schools and churches.

"The harshest criticism came from our own families. They wondered if we knew what we were doing; they assured us there would be nothing but problems raising a black child. Of course we knew what we were doing! That's why I got so sick on the trip to Wyoming. We realized we were both approaching forty; we had to think of our other three children who would also feel the ostracism if it came to that; we knew we wanted to allow this child to explore his three cultures and identify with them. It was no small task we had undertaken. We had fear and trembling because we *did* know what we were doing. And this was before we became aware of the learning disability, which presented a whole different set of problems, unrelated to race. But we also knew what parenthood was all about, and we had a glimpse into our own abilities to raise children. We believed that if anyone could undertake this task, we could." Alli noticed Marilyn's determined jaw.

"How did your other children handle having a new baby brother of a different race?" asks Kate.

Marilyn answered, "They dearly loved him from the very first day. He always amazed us, so the older children were constantly telling stories about what Jeff did."

"Marilyn, the question of white families adopting black, Hispanic, or Native American children is currently a very controversial one. Some states don't even allow a white family to adopt a child of a different culture. How do you feel about this?" Alli asks, observing the interest in Marilyn's story.

"We feel strongly that a child should stay with their own race, if possible. It certainly is easier to identify with your own culture if both parents and children are of the same race. If a black, Hispanic, or Native American family had had an adoption application on file at the time we got Jeff, they would have been chosen ahead of us. Rightfully so. Since that didn't happen, we are his parents. Not only did he come to us with three cultures of his own, but he also has the Norwegian and Swedish nationalities of his parents to claim. What a diverse mixture he has grown up with! This little guy sat in his high chair eating lutefisk!!"

Laughing with the others, Sally says, "He probably also says Uff-da!"

"Especially when he's eating lutefisk!" comes a quick reply.

Smiling, Marilyn continues. "This baby deserved a loving home from the beginning. We wish they had found us before 2-1/2 months went by!"

"Are you leading into something on the learning disability?" asks Alli who is well informed about such disabilities from her college studies.

"Yes. Jeff's learning disability wasn't discovered until he was about four. I'm a kindergarten teacher, so I was well aware that children take an interest in learning to write their names at this age. Jeff couldn't do it. He physically could not write. Not being knowledgeable about learning disabilities at the time, we were confused about what was wrong and what we could do about it.

"While studying for my master's degree in early childhood education, I learned what sometimes causes learning disabilities. Babies need stimulation to the brain at critical times early in their lives: within days, weeks, months of birth. This stimulation is brought about by stroking, touching, cuddling. You know how instinctively a parent strokes a baby's head and body, touching it, cuddling it, kissing it. When a baby has this kind of touching stimulation at those very early, critical times in their lives, they feel assured that someone is there to take care of them. Learning their caretaker's voice is important, too. If a baby's need for this kind of stimulation is not met, he goes on without that development.

"This kind of stimulation was missing in Jeff's very early life, and possibly his learning disability is the result. Obviously I can't prove my theory, but it's a feeling I have about his handicap. Much research has been done on this topic, so I have references to back up my theory."

"Thanks so much, Marilyn. I know you 're planning to talk more about this topic of learning disabilities for a later chapter. We'll allow you to rest for awhile now!" Alli decides that her first impression of Marilyn is pretty accurate. She's another very impressive lady.

When Adopted Children Seek Their Birth Mothers

"How would you react if your adopted child wanted to find his birth mother?" asks Alli. "This seems to be a current trend."

Audrey begins. "From the time they were small, we made our children aware that they were adopted children. Once they comprehended this, we didn't continually remind them of it. We raised them as 'ours' but if our children, now adults, want to explore their roots for curiosity or for medical reasons, I feel that they certainly have a right to do that. We loved them and raised them to the best of our ability, so their feeling of being part of our family will always be with them."

"We also told our boys that they were adopted," says Kate, "even before they could understand what the word meant. It was cute though, when people would see the three boys together—two adopted and one biological—and say, 'You guys are brothers? You surely don't look alike.' One had blue eyes, dark hair; another had brown eyes, dark curly hair, and the third had blue eyes, blonde hair. The boys didn't bother to explain, but they would tell me about it later, and they were amused.

"As for searching out their biological parents, the boys have always known that they can find out if they want to because South Dakota law allows adopted children to look at their records when they reach age 21. But so far our young adults have shown no interest. We've been told that girls are more interested in pursuing this than boys. Both of our boys were born to college students. In both instances, the mother felt that she could not marry the father. Each mother felt that the best thing for her child was to give up the baby for adoption to a family better able to care for him and love him. I think our boys have a good feeling toward their biological parents because of that, but they don't have a driving need to find out any more about them. The mother of Sterling, our first son, wrote a letter asking that he be adopted into a family with other children. She's an artist, and our son excels in art. The father of our second son was a concert pianist, and Pierce excels in music. Our two adopted children are both very gifted with these unique talents. I can vouch for the fact that parents love their children the same whether they are adopted or biological."

Alli asks Marilyn, "Have you encouraged Jeff to learn more about his birth parents, or would you rather he not pursue that information?"

"We have encouraged Jeff to seek out his birth parents," Marilyn answers, "but so far he has shown no interest. One reason we have suggested this is to learn his medical history. Recently we found out that he has high cholesterol, and we wished we knew something about his parents' medical background."

Audrey has another point to make on this topic. "One fairly new development in adoption proceedings is for the birth mother to choose who will be her baby's adoptive parents. I have mixed feelings about this. I think that it would be confusing for a child to grow up with a birth mother and adoptive parents, especially if the birth mother keeps in touch."

"Yes, I agree," says Alli. "If she keeps in touch, I wonder what role this birth mother plays in the life of the child as he or she grows up."

Alli continues. "Ladies, I can't begin to tell you how much I'm learning from you. Your directness, your wisdom, and your practical insights will have a permanent effect on me.

"Thank you for this wonderful education on pregnancy, miscarriages, adoption, and living life to its fullest."

Audrey says, "Alli, you are so much like your mother. We all see the resemblance. I feel like I'm in a time warp, and Marion is here discussing these topics. We're so happy you came to our lakeside reunion. I enjoy seeing you referring to the posters you made from the '56 yearbook."

Alli sighs and says, "What a privilege it is for me to be in your midst. Let's take a lunch break before two of the women talk about two very special children and two very special families."

5

Very Special Children
Need Very Special Families

His Mama's Gift

A summer-jammied little boy
    squats toward three dandelions
    still wet under morning sun.

Fingers innocent and curious
    brush warm dew from petals
    soft and fragile
      —and he smiles.

Three yellow velvet faces
    smile toward him
    as he grasps them

    wet dirt trailing
    from their roots.

He turns and he dances
    with his golden bouquet,
    his precious hand-hugged gift

    made for mama's smile.

© Daphne Lewis

Alli continues guiding our dialogue. "Moving to the next topic, another concern of mothers is the health of the baby God has given them. Every mother wants a strong and healthy child, but God sometimes grants a very special child whose mental or physical capacity is somewhat diminished or limited, but whose ability to love and be loved is extraordinary. Renae and Claudia have had experiences with their very special children and their very special families."

Earlier Alli had categorized Renae as the world traveler who had put marriage on the back burner until she got the wanderlust out of her veins. Now she sees this determined lady with her short, gray, wavy hair, looking over her glasses at the group. Alli senses she is in for another dramatic learning experience.

Travis—A Very Special Child

Renae had written notes in advance to ensure the chronology of events. Alli invites her to proceed.

"We were living in Italy in 1970, the year Travis was born. The nearest major military hospital was in Wiesbaden, Germany, so it was there I went a week before his due date. (This same hospital provided care for the hostages after their release from the Middle East.) Going to Wiesbaden was like going home, since we had lived there three years earlier. To avoid a long weekend stay in the hospital, we flew back to Italy when Travis was only two days old.

"Travis seemed perfectly normal at birth. Gradually we began to notice that he did not suck well, and he rarely cried; he frequently yelled out as though he was very frightened. When this happened, the only way to calm him was for Jerry to walk briskly up and down the hallway, cuddling, patting, and comforting him until Travis suddenly stopped yelling. Travis seemed to be fascinated by light, but responded very little to noise.

"When his first birthday arrived, Travis was back in the hospital for evaluation. After numerous tests and comparisons were completed, it was determined that he had the classic indications for Noonan's Syndrome. Once again the military hospital provided us with a wonderful staff and services. One of the doctors had seen a case like this before and, surprisingly, that baby boy also had red curly hair, just like Travis.

"Explaining all the identifying characteristics, the doctor wanted to be sure we clearly understood what was involved. He told us Travis would probably be short, and he would be slow in developing both physically and mentally. The prognosis was not a complete surprise to us, but it took a little while for the finality of the doctor's words to soak in. Back at the hotel, I sat on the edge of the bed and cried. Jerry reassured me that things would work out. He felt confident we could handle whatever came our way.

"Finding the cause of Travis's condition was important to us at this particular time, since I was pregnant again. Our doctor emphasized the time element, because if there were a serious hereditary condition also afflicting the unborn child, he felt we should be allowed to consider abortion. Genetic testing indicated there was no chromosomal abnormality and that our chances of having a second child with a similar condition were no greater than for any other 36-year-old woman. Fortunately, we were not faced with a decision of terminating this pregnancy. But from this experience, I feel that such a decision is one that should be made by the couple in consultation with their doctor.

"Every routine event in Travis's life, whether it was rolling over, sitting up, or walking, became a milestone. He was 4 years old before he could walk alone. As an adult, he still needs to be bathed, have his teeth brushed, and be shaved. With assistance he can dress himself. His mental age is that of a pre-schooler.

"I returned to the United States when Travis was 18 months old. I was several months pregnant when I left Italy ahead of Jerry. That was a memorable trip! I flew from Southern Italy to Minnesota, via New York, with a 6 year old, an 18 month old not yet able to walk, and my pregnant body retaining fluids. I looked like a blimp about to give birth! It was hot and humid. No doubt fellow travelers felt uneasy around me. Let me tell you—my parents were a mighty welcome sight when I reached Moorhead.

"The doctor's early prediction that Travis would be short was accurate. Small for his age and mentally handicapped, people often assumed Travis was much younger than he was. Because of this, we were able to leave him in a Sunday morning church nursery or in military nurseries at an older age than the other children. Those short respites were helpful to me since Travis didn't sit still very long and couldn't be left alone for any length of time. Later we worked out an arrangement with my mother on Sunday mornings. She kept Travis while we attended early church services; then she went to a later service.

"School for Travis began at age 2-1/2 and continued until age 21. He has had excellent programs all along the way. In New York we lived on base, where our son, Andy, attended school. There were no birth to age four programs available for Travis in the area. An evaluation of Travis at the Albany Medical Center revealed he also had autistic tendencies. Avoiding eye contact, he was often in his own world with a certain disregard for external reality. We also were told to watch closely for seizures but, fortunately, they never occurred.

"A year after arriving in New York, Jerry received orders for an assignment in Turkey. We contacted the late then-U. S. Senator Hubert Humphrey of Minnesota for assistance in having Jerry's orders changed. Because of Travis's condition, we didn't feel we could go back overseas at this point. Within a few weeks, Jerry had orders to report to Virginia, and Travis had a space reserved for him at a special school in Arlington.

"While stationed in Virginia, we had 3-year-old Travis's hearing tested at Walter Reed Hospital. Diagnosed with a significant hearing loss, he was fitted with binaural hearing aids. He kept pulling them off. Within a short time, he also needed glasses, so we had the hearing aids attached to the glasses. He was more content to leave them in place. He wore this combination until he was 6 years old, when it was finally determined that he no longer needed glasses and his hearing was normal or near normal. He must have been relieved to be rid of this headgear.

"After a year in Virginia, Jerry got orders to the Philippines. Since there were no programs for Travis over there, the kids and I moved back to Minnesota. Jerry served two years there and then retired. Those two years were difficult without a husband/father to assist with the children, but my mother was a tremendous help to me. Had it not been so important for Travis to have a routine in his life, Jerry may have stayed with the Air Force for a few more years.

"Travis is not able to talk. He can yell, but he has never said a word. When frustrated or when taken where he doesn't want to be, Travis can yell *very* loudly. A regular daily schedule is something he needs to keep him on course. When I was a substitute teacher in his classroom, he was really confused. In his mind, I could not be his mother and also be his teacher, so I discontinued substituting in that capacity.

"One year Travis stayed with a foster family in Detroit Lakes, Minnesota. The husband and wife were both professionals in special education. What started out as a summer in foster care continued for a whole year because they provided such a good environment for him. It was also a wonderful respite for us. During this year, he was introduced to sign language which has become his main method of communication. He has built a fairly large vocabulary in signing.

"Programs in special education have been excellent. Travis began in a Growth and Development Center while we were in Virginia. He had assistance from specialists in gross motor and fine motor development and from physical and occupational therapists. In Minnesota, he has been in special education through age 21. We have had the support of school staff and specialists as well as social service agencies and respite-care programs. There is a lot of help available, but it doesn't come knocking at your door. We had to seek out every avenue, gradually becoming aware of available assistance. Through the Association for Retarded Citizens, we have kept informed of the agencies we need to contact for support services.

"Now at age 21, Travis's education is over. Graduation was a time of uncertainty for us because we knew the daily routine had ended. We worried about how Travis would cope with a new environment. It was also necessary for us to let go. He now lives in an apartment with another young man with special needs, away from an overly helpful mom and dad. Living with another person cuts down on Travis's demands for individual attention.

"Social workers try to find appropriate work for him, enabling him to get out into the community and even earn a little money. In addition, they try to keep continuity in his program by scheduling activities such as movies, shopping, and clothes washing on certain days. He learns what to expect—not because it is Monday or Tuesday, but because it's the day after each event. It does help. We remain Travis's legal guardians and, in that capacity, we meet with the staff on a quarterly basis to give input and get feedback on how he is doing.

When he sees us, he gets excited and laughs. Seeing his happy reaction is so rewarding for Jerry and me.

"We get wonderful feedback on Travis. Most people who work with him comment on the challenge he has presented and the joy it has been. Others cannot understand or figure out what he wants. We understand perfectly! We were frustrated plenty of times; and so was Travis! Jerry and I seemed to develop a sixth sense as to when we needed to step in and take over during the most exasperating times. Travis can be a tease, but he treats others well and accepts the people who care for him.

Reflections

"Travis has always been first of all a joy and delight, and secondly, a challenge! He is healthy; he does not suffer, and he is not aware that he has special needs. Nor can he consciously understand that there is a God who watches over him and cares for him. I do. He is constantly in my prayers. Our pastor once said: 'For every God-given challenge there is God-given strength.'

"Having a child like Travis requires his family to adopt a life style that is quite different from other families. It was difficult to take him to public places because he couldn't sit still, and he would yell loudly at inappropriate times. Nor was it easy to entertain guests in our own home. Although willing to play with toys, Travis also liked to snack. He demanded a lot of attention, which interrupted any visiting we might attempt with guests.

"When one child in a family requires so much of the parents' attention, the other children are often taken for granted. Your handicapped child comes first, and the other children often sacrifice their special time with mom and dad. At times, it was hard for Andy and Jenny because we weren't always able to be there for them. If they were ever embarrassed about their brother, they didn't complain. Only a couple of times did one of them say that Travis had prevented our family from doing something they really wanted to do. As a result of having Travis as a brother, they have developed more understanding and compassion for mentally-handicapped people.

"Living with a challenge of this nature on a daily basis sometimes causes tension in a marriage. But our marriage has been strengthened by it. We shared equally in bathing, dressing, and helping Travis eat. Jerry has more patience and endurance than I, but we were a source of strength for each other in the most difficult times. And, we receive strength every day from God."

As Renae completes her prepared notes, Alli asks how her life has changed now that Travis is no longer living at home.

"For the first time in our lives we have the luxury of coming and going on a whim—no planning is necessary. Except for the routine of our jobs, we can decide on a moment's notice to go somewhere. We are enjoying that."

"Thanks, Renae. These special children must have special parents like you," suggests Alli.

Renae comments, "Parents who have a child with a developmental disability often suffer from what sociologist Simon Olshansky calls 'chronic sorrow.' These sorrowful feelings are normal because of the long-term implications for the entire family. It doesn't mean that parents don't love or feel pride in their child. Belonging to a support group of people who have lived through the experience can be very helpful."

Alli explains that she has studied about developmental disabilities in her psychology classes. "My heart goes out to Renae, as I observe the strength she exemplifies.

Even though she experiences chronic sorrow, Renae doesn't wallow in self-pity, but draws on God-given strength to make the best possible life for her handicapped son." Alli smiles at this small, be-spectacled, neat-as-a-pin woman. Another new friend!

As Alli turns to Claudia for her story, she realizes she has come to know this woman quite well. During all the kind invitations to dinner or dessert on the patio, Claudia has listened to Alli agonize about her job, discuss her friends, even decide on a graduate school. It dawns on Alli that these are the same topics she'd discuss with her mother—if she were living. Claudia is quiet, ambitious, and hard working. She's also well organized, as evidenced by the typewritten manuscript she's holding— the pre-written story of her daughter. Alli is aware that Claudia's daughter, Stephanie, who died at age seven, would be just a year older than she is. As Alli prepares to listen to her new friend, she notices again the ever-present blue-rimmed glasses and the high-lighted gray in her blonde hair.

Seven Years With Stephanie

"We lost Stephanie, our fourth child and only daughter, at the age of seven from a rare disease of the central nervous system. The disease was never diagnosed. Her illness began when she was 2-1/2 years old and lasted for 4-1/2 years. She became completely paralyzed, mute and, later, blind. Because she couldn't respond, it was hard toward the end to tell if she might possibly be deaf as well.

"Like a slow virus, the disease came on gradually, and we were not aware of anything being wrong for several months. In looking back, we would think of some particular behavior that wasn't typical and wondered if something had been going on long before we realized it. The major brain damage happened within a period of about six weeks when she was rendered paralyzed and mute. It was May and June of 1968.

"Since the age of 18 months, Stephanie had been treated for a congenitally dislocated hip—her left one—and had been through two 'frog-leg' casts; she was wearing a brace that also held her legs outward. The brace was removed for periods of time during the day, and she was encouraged to crawl to strengthen her legs.

"Not able to walk at a time when most other children walk, Stephanie's energies were instead channelled into learning to talk. In a heavy cast and an awkward frog-leg position, she had to be tied into an armless chair or positioned on the sofa, always with a stack of pillows under the cast. As I kept her near me and conversed with her, Stephanie's speech developed. By age 2, her speech had advanced into fairly long sentences.

"Learning to tell a joke brought lots of attention from her brothers. Because they thought it was hilarious, she got a lot of practice as an entertainer by saying: "Why did the elephant sit on the marshmallow?" Then answering her own question: "So he wouldn't fall in the cocoa!" We saw a delightful personality developing.

"Perhaps 18 months was late to discover that congenital hip problem, but nevertheless that's what happened. I have since become aware of a procedure done at birth to check for dislocation. But until she was trying to stand alone and couldn't balance, we had no idea anything was wrong. She could walk sideways around the bed.

"Hindsight is 20/20 and makes us wonder why we didn't realize something else was wrong at the time. I remember one fleeting thought while changing her diaper: that her left leg seemed shorter than her right one.

However, the thought was immediately dismissed because I decided the old sagging bathinette was playing tricks on my eyes.

"Looking back and thinking about our failure to discover the dislocated hip right after birth has made me wonder if this was part of the whole scheme of things, part of God's plan for our daughter's short life. Unable to develop a sense of independence because she had to be carried everywhere, she instead developed complete trust in us as her caregivers. This trust was crucial when she became paralyzed and totally dependent on us.

"Moving along the floor, with or without the brace, required strength in her arms and shoulders. She would put her head down on the carpet to rest when her arms got tired. Visiting the grandparents the Christmas before she became ill, we noticed her eyes were swollen and red, even swelling up as we were looking at her. Thinking she might be having an allergic reaction, we talked about taking her to the emergency room, but we didn't do it when the swelling disappeared. On the trip home, a 500-mile drive, she cried the entire time. A bed was made for her in the back seat so she could sleep comfortably with the brace on. Sitting beside her on the way home, I gave her baby aspirin and tried to comfort her, but this did not relieve the pain she must have been feeling. Motion sickness had never been a problem in the past, if, indeed that was the problem. The trip was a nightmare. Once again, hindsight suggested it was the beginning of the disease or that she had picked up a virus—an observation made later by a pediatrician. Everything seemed back to normal after we got home.

"We knew something was wrong when she would wake up from her nap and continue to lie in her crib quietly rather than calling out in her baby talk, *'Mommy, my 'wate' up!'* She was losing her ability to speak. She also was losing strength and coordination in her arms and hands, and feeding herself was obviously difficult. All of this was happening in such a short time frame that we were totally baffled by what was going on. Within six weeks, she was completely paralyzed and mute. Believe me, a lot of prayers were said and a lot of tears were shed in the midst of this confusion.

"Our local doctors were puzzled by her disease. The first doctor who saw her early-on thought it was probably psychological and once her hip correction was completed she would be okay. Later, when he learned of the seriousness of the disease, he called to apologize. I appreciated his caring.

"We were referred to a pediatric specialist at a medical school hospital. He also seemed to be puzzled, but I remember him saying, 'It's terminal.' I felt completely intimidated by this older man with his heavy German accent who, I'm sure, was brilliant and had excellent credentials. But, he wasn't very personable. At that time, I was not familiar with medical terminology, so I could only guess that saying 'It's terminal' was the medical way of saying, 'She's going to die.' What nobody could have told us was that death would be a slow process, going on for more than four years.

"Hospice wasn't available at that time, but some type of nursing assistance would have been very helpful. In the beginning it was not terribly difficult to care for her; but as her disease progressed, it became harder. Part of the difficulty was in handling a limp body about three feet long, which needed support all over and could not hold on to me. It was hard to bathe her and feed her, especially when she was not able to swallow easily. Each feeding took an hour or two. After a time, she was just not getting enough to eat; she was losing weight. Her little seat became folds of skin.

"Finally the doctor put her on a feeding tube, and she was fed a special liquid formula. They taught me how to insert the tube, which went into her nose and down to her stomach. This happened a year and a half before she died. After seeing the results, I wished we had started feeding her this way sooner, but the doctor kept insisting it was a last resort thing to do. She began gaining weight from the very first feeding and had a contented look on her face like a tiny baby who has just been fed.

"Knowing we had an awesome task in providing care for her, we prayed for strength every day; and we felt our prayers were answered. Although not in any pain from the disease, she did need phenobarbital to prevent seizures. As the disease worsened for another two years and the optic nerve was affected, she became blind. Several times throughout her illness, she was hospitalized, usually for pneumonia.

"On one occasion about ten months before Stephanie died, a nurse came in to check on her and decided to change her diaper. As I sat there watching, the nurse lifted Stephanie's long legs straight up in the air as though changing the diaper of a newborn or a very small baby. She should not have done it that way. My method was to gently slide the diaper under her buttocks leaving her legs alone. Although Stephanie hadn't been able to really respond for some time, the expression on her face at this moment showed very definite pain or shock. I was alarmed at the nurse's insensitivity but, being easily intimidated, I didn't say anything.

"The next day, an area on her left thigh was swollen; the doctor ordered x-rays. She had a broken leg. Because Stephanie had never walked, her bones had atrophied to a point where they were easy to break. X-rays also were difficult to read because of that atrophy. Following this episode, the doctors gave a lecture to the medical staff as to the importance of being extremely careful with patients whose bones were as fragile as Stephanie's. Interestingly enough, we were never charged for that hospital stay and our insurance company was never billed. Perhaps we had grounds for a lawsuit but, in 1972, we didn't even think of it. Our actions today might be different.

"Stephanie died on December 4, 1972, three weeks before Christmas. It was a Monday, and it was her brother's tenth birthday. The immediate cause of her death was pneumonia, just as the doctors had predicted some time earlier. When she began showing signs of congestion and running a temperature of 104, we bundled her up in a blanket and took her to the clinic where the doctor prescribed some medicine. As he always said at times like this, 'If she isn't better by tomorrow, we will have to put her in the hospital.'

"Back home we made her as comfortable as possible and started medication given through the feeding tube. Her breathing was quite labored, causing her chest to rise and fall.

"Since Elliot had a birthday that day, I baked and frosted a cake while running back and forth to the bedroom checking on Stephanie and giving her the hourly dose of medicine. When the birthday cake was frosted, mindful of keeping an eye on the clock, I gathered up the medicine and syringe and headed to the bedroom for the 3 p.m. dosage. Although I had known for 4-1/2 years that my daughter was going to die, the thought that she might die that day had not occurred to me.

"At the precise moment my foot touched the bedroom floor, I experienced something that can only be described as an explosion within my mind. The words 'She's dead!' filled my head. Startled, I hesitated momentarily, looking up. The explosion in my mind came from above. No voices. No lights. I didn't see any person or any image, yet I firmly believe God was there at that moment. From the bedroom doorway, I couldn't see

Stephanie in the crib; but I have always felt that God was preparing me for what I was to find. Perhaps she died at that moment.

"Getting to the crib, I set the medicine on the chest of drawers, freeing my hands. Stephanie was lying very still. Opening the robe she was wearing, I saw her chest, which had been heaving with each breath, was silent now. I put my hand there. It was so warm and so quiet. My mind was reacting illogically because I began thinking that it didn't matter if she wasn't breathing since people can live without breathing. She could not be dead. Then I realized I could not feel a heartbeat. I still didn't think she could be dead.

"My own heart was pounding as I ran to the telephone to call the doctor. Halfway to the phone, I decided she could not be dead, and he would think I was crazy, so I went back to check again. Nothing had changed.

"When I told the doctor I thought she might be dead, his reply was 'Could be.' He came to the house within a matter of minutes. In the meantime, I called Martin at work.

"In some ways a sense of relief came over me when Stephanie died. When someone you love is desperately ill, can never be well, and whose body has become a prison for them, death really is a victory. A lot of people have experienced that feeling—the letting go and the sense of peace knowing that their loved one is at last free from their affliction. Maybe the letting go is easier for those of us whose loved ones have been sick for a long time than it is for people who lose a loved one in an accident or a very sudden illness.

"Or maybe not. Maybe it's just that a person is in the process of letting go gradually while their loved one is slowly dying. People who lose a loved one suddenly have to let go after the death takes place, and it might seem to take longer that way. And it might seem more difficult, especially losing a healthy person in an accident. No doubt, our family went through some stages of grief before Stephanie died, knowing she would never be well."

Alli shudders at the mention of sudden death in an accident, but she manages to say, "Stephanie was your youngest child. How did her illness and death affect your other children?"

Reflections

"From their earliest memories of her, she was ill. The boys were helpful and protective of their sister. We always tried to have Stephanie near us wherever we were in the house to lessen her fears of being left alone. Because she was completely paralyzed, we used a stroller folded into a bed to move her around inside the house. This way she could be beside the table when we ate our meals; she could be in the kitchen with me or in the living room when we were there. When the boys came home from school, they would spend some time talking to her or reading to her. Even though she could not respond, she was aware.

"During the years of her illness, Martin and I knew it was terminal and that she would probably die of pneumonia. Somehow I thought the boys knew this, too; but I don't recall that we actually explained everything to them. Looking back, I realize it was a mistake not to be deliberate in our discussion with the boys about what the future held for Stephanie. At the time I didn't realize how uninformed they were. Only recently, I learned that they didn't understand what was happening. They thought Stephanie would grow up but would always be in a crib because she was paralyzed.

"Something else I learned recently: Eric, at age 11, cried himself to sleep many nights after Stephanie died, praying that God would bring her back and take him instead. He had known for years how happy I was to have a daughter after three sons; now it seemed terribly unfair to him that I no longer had a daughter."

"What a caring son and brother," Audrey suggests.

"Having a terminally-ill child in a home keeps parents focused on the needs of that child sometimes to the exclusion of your other children. The length of Stephanie's illness may have been a factor in neglecting to keep the other children informed of what was happening. Everything was happening so slowly. A short-term illness becomes a day-to-day vigil, but a long-term illness becomes more a way of life. In retrospect, I think we made a lot of mistakes coping with the situation as it affected each family member."

Kate counsels, "Don't blame yourself. Remember, 20 years ago there was little assistance for families in your situation. Hospice wasn't available. Counseling for families with a terminally-ill loved one was unusual. People were expected to be strong and deal with a crises themselves. You did that."

"Yes, I think we did our best, with God's help. Our son, Eric, and his wife just had their first child—a boy born brain damaged due to a hydrocephalic condition. After the initial shock and emotional trauma of such news, Eric said he could deal with his son's uncertain future because he remembers our family life with a handicapped child. It was heartwarming to hear that."

A Christmas Funeral

Claudia says, "Stephanie's funeral was beautiful. The older children from the Christian Day School, which our boys attended, sang *Children of the Heavenly Father*. Whenever we sing that in church, I get choked-up. The pastor had such a wonderful message. We decided to use it in our Christmas letter that year so we could tell our friends in a heartfelt way about Stephanie's death. I'd like to include a small portion of that sermon:

> *The story is told of two strangers, a small boy and an older man, who were fishing from the banks of the Mississippi River. Though the fishing was poor, by the time the sun began to set, they had talked of many things. Just at dusk a large river boat was seen moving slowly in the distance. When the boy saw the boat he began to shout and wave his arms, that he might attract the attention of those on the boat.*
>
> *The man watched for some time and then said: "Son, you are foolish if you think that boat is going to stop for you. It's on its way to some unknown place and it surely won't stop for a small boy." But suddenly the boat began to slow down, and it moved toward the river bank. To the man's amazement, the boat come near enough to the shore that a gangplank was lowered and the boy, ready to enter the boat, turned to his friend and said: "I am not foolish, Mister. You see, my father is the captain of this boat and we are going to a new home up the river."...*
>
> *Life is full of unscheduled stops along the river of life and these stops cause pain and grief that at times border on the unbearable. And yet we bear them, because in faith we continue to believe that our Father in heaven is the captain of that boat. And because he is the captain, the boat is headed for a new home. Death is not the end of life; it is the beginning of a new adventure upon the river of life....*
>
> Pastor Durwood Buchheim

"Since the funeral was three weeks before Christmas, the church was decorated, and I have a picture in my mind of a little white casket topped with a spray of red and white carnations and greens, Christmas colors, standing beside the decorated Christmas tree. The casket spray also had a feathery white dove on it, and we have used that white dove on the top of our Christmas tree every year since Stephanie died as a memorial to her and an acceptance of her eternal peace."

Reaching for a tissue, Alli invites comments, adding, "What a touching and love-filled story, Claudia."

"Claudia, I remember your Christmas letter that year, and it was just beautiful," says Dana. "Parents might wonder why they were given one of these very special children. I wonder if God chose Claudia and Renae to mother these children because they are both so loving and patient."

"I remember that letter, too; I used parts of it several times in Bible studies, especially the little story you just read. It is so touching," Audrey adds.

Claudia concludes her story. "Carolers were at our home the evening after the funeral, standing outside in the snow singing *Silent Night, Holy Night*. One line in that Christmas Carol has taken on a new and comforting meaning for me:

'Sleep in heavenly peace.'"

6

Family Life...Sometimes There Are Tribulations

A Mother's Psalm

My child, you are in those turbulent teen years—
What will happen now?
  I grieve, in thought, as though you had already
    Suffered
    and caused others pain as well.

My child, know how to recognize evil—
So that your innocence and trust
will not make you a
    Victim
    needing years to overcome.

My child, know your changing body—
Give it respect, as God intended.
It is not a toy for someone elses'
    Pleasure—
    not meant for teenage parenthood.

My child, know who your companions are—
The best friends share your time
as well as family values.
    Peer pressure
    can sometimes be one's downfall.

My child, know the deadly substances
   available for teens
   to inhale or consume.
      Addiction
      is not a pleasant way to live.

My child, know that youthful rebellion
   is often an expression
   of wanting to be
      Recognized—
      Calmly help us see your point of view.

My child, know that your parents love you—
   Even when angry words are spoken
   because we don't fully
      Understand
      the logic of the teenage mind.

My child, know the God who loves you—
   Allow Him to lead the way.
   These years, instead of turbulent, can be
      Gentle,
      when walking in His steps.

© Carol Wade Lee

"Life after graduation seemed like you were entering the Promised Land—marriage, vocation, your own families. None of you became ground hogs after graduation, living in some burrow under that Promised Land. Instead, you've dwelt on its productive plains, been on a mountain top or two, and in valleys. When family members were led into the far country of alcoholism, drug abuse, and other painful difficulties, it is clear you were like the Waiting Father in the Biblical parable. Never giving up, your hearts reached out across deep rifts and through great pain. You agreed to discuss the thorny times, in the hope of being a help to other people."

The women are quite taken by Alli's eloquence as she gets organized for this next conversation.

"Like most American families, your experiences raising children have been both rewarding and exasperating. Christian families are definitely not exempt from the darker influences in our society, and you have shared some of your worries and concerns about behaviors of your teenager or adult children, as well as other family members. Many Christian parents can relate to your feelings about alcohol and drug use, cohabitation, and life without the church."

Families Touched by Alcoholism

"Someone referred to alcohol as the 'demon' in a loved one with this disease," continues Alli. "However, when we begin to regard alcoholism as a demon, we are not using the word as a figure of speech any longer. But is it an exaggeration?"

Claudia responds firmly. Alli knew there had been a problem, but she was stunned by Claudia's sense of resolve. "Daily living for an alcoholic's family means dealing with a demon. Our family has known the impact of alcoholism. I call it a demon because its mood-altering effect and addictiveness can turn an otherwise gentle and wonderful person into someone we don't know. The ripple effect of drinking causes so much heartache; so many other people are affected by one person's behavior.

"Our son's alcoholism was not obvious to us because he was very careful to avoid his parents when he had been drinking. He knew we would disapprove. He also knew we respected his privacy, his 'space' (which he took advantage of). Martin and I were both raised in families where drinking was feared, not merely frowned upon. The pioneer generation of Norwegians included a large percentage who had the same genetic enzyme problem with alcohol that many Native Americans have. In that first generation, far too many Norwegian immigrants literally drank themselves to death. So yes, our prairie culture often includes a deathly *fear* of alcohol. We raised our children in the same kind of atmosphere in which we grew up. It never occurred to me that our sons would drink.

"There was alcoholism in my family, however. My brothers. My grandfather also was an alcoholic. Back in the early 1900s, he drank whenever he drove his team of horses to town for supplies. He always made it home again, because once he got into the horse-driven wagon, the horses knew the way back.

"Elliot's involvement with alcohol started in high school, but, like many other parents, we were blind to our son's activities. Everyone was working in our family, including the boys. They developed their own schedules, so we didn't have very many meals together or quality family time. We were a classic example of so many families these days, everyone going in a different direction. Martin and I paid dearly for our failure to insist on family time.

"To say that teenage rebellion is hard to deal with is an understatement. Some children feel obligated to reject parental standards and their own upbringing. Our children convinced themselves that since their parents didn't drink, they were definitely *going* to drink."

And so...

"Elliot's drinking patterns got out of hand when he joined a college fraternity. Not only did these young people consume lots of beer, but, tragically, they also rationalized that it was okay to use drugs—marijuana and cocaine. During the summer of '85, Elliot worked at his cousin's ranch. While he was there, his cousin recognized Elliot's alcohol problem and convinced him he needed treatment. This came as a shock to me. His cousin knew of a treatment center at a nearby hospital, with an in-patient 28-day program. Elliot was willing to be admitted. We talked to the counselors by phone and made the necessary arrangements. All of the counselors are recovering alcoholics or former drug abusers.

"We were told it was a four-week program and during the third week, family week, we were encouraged to come there and participate. We were able to take time off from our jobs to go.

"About two days before we were going to drive the 800 miles to attend family week, one of the counselors called me. Elliot had been in to see him and was threatening to quit the program if we attended family week. It was apparent to the counselor that Elliot was hiding something, and walking away from treatment was his easy out.

"Since he was making progress, I didn't want to see him walk out of treatment. Continuing to talk to Elliot, the counselor convinced Elliot to stay on for family week. The counselor had determined that Elliot was willing to acknowledge he is an alcoholic, but admitting to using cocaine on several occasions was something else.

"From my entry-level understanding of psychology, I believed he could admit to alcoholism because there were other alcoholics in our extended family. But there were no 'drug' addicts in the family, so admitting to cocaine use would be devastating. He didn't want us to know. By now it had been several months since he used cocaine, and he did not use it again."

Alli hurts for her friend and injects, "This had to be a heart-breaking ordeal for you, Claudia." All of a sudden, Alli feels guilty that she has laid so many of her problems on Claudia's doorstep.

Claudia continues. "Yes, but now there was hope, since he was in treatment. Family week was certainly an eye opener. Participants who started the same week as Elliot had by now become friends. They were spending all of their waking hours together: eating, attending small sessions, talking about their addictions, going to group lectures, or watching TV during free time—and smoking. I was amazed by how much they all smoked. The program could concentrate on helping a person give up only one addiction at a time.

"Quite a cross-section of people was present in the program during that four-week period. There was Harold, an elderly man who had been through treatment several times; Gary, a 30-something husband and father who had support from his wife and children, as well as from his parents and brothers; Monica, a middle-aged woman who was addicted to prescription drugs; Rudy, a young male Native American; Mona, a woman in her twenties whose mother had gone through the treatment program earlier in her life. The most heart-breaking of all was Julie, a petite, pretty fifteen year old who could be anybody's darling daughter—but she was an alcoholic. Julie had the support of her mother and her mother's female friend.

"During one of the open lectures by the program director, we sat near Julie. Through humor and animation, the director was effective at getting his point across. He asked the patients a general question concerning what they worry about. My heart went out to Julie when I overheard her say, to nobody in particular, 'I worry every month about being pregnant!'"

"You mentioned small groups. How did they function?" Alli asks as she thinks back to her own education.

"Three or four patients along with their family members made up these groups. The three of us were in a group with Julie and her support; Gary, the 30-something husband with his supportive family, and Mona, with her mother.

"Each group session began with the patient acknowledging some alcohol- or drug-related activity in which he or she had been involved before treatment. Then he or she had to explain to the group why this activity was hazardous. Each patient had to identify himself or herself by first name and include the words, 'I am a drug-addicted alcoholic.' To reinforce in their own minds that they were, indeed, alcoholics, this type of identification was repeated at every introduction.

"On the third day, these small group sessions became family encounter sessions. Arranged in a circle, the group watched as each family member took a turn sitting in the middle of the circle facing their loved one who was the patient. Earlier that day, we were given an assignment to jot down questions we wanted to ask our family member—questions having to do with alcohol-related behavior or hurts caused by drinking. In return, the patients were allowed to confront their family members with similar statements pertaining to hurts they had suffered when their loved ones had belittled, rebuked, or rejected them because of their drinking. It was a two-way street—a very emotional two-way street—and everyone shed some tears."

"Exactly what was the purpose of these encounters?" inquires Alli.

"It was a tool the counselors used in their assessment of the family. While the encounter was taking place, the counselors and others in the outer circle observed the interaction between the two family members in the middle of the circle. If the counselors believed the family member was too forgiving toward the patient, or not forgiving enough, or resigned to the alcoholic's behavior, they would point this out. Or if they felt the patient was uncooperative or was blaming his bad behavior on someone or something other than alcohol, the counselors pointed this out.

"When our turn came, Martin went into the center first and proceeded with our list of questions. Listening to him ask every question on the list, I hoped they would just skip me and not expect both father and mother to go through the encounter. It didn't work that way. When he returned to the outer circle, they motioned for me to go into the center to face my son. What was I going to ask?

"I followed up on a couple of questions Martin had asked, so Elliot could hear my reaction. Elliot recalled some parenting faults, when he perceived he had been punished unfairly. His father and I both apologized for any hurt we had caused him.

"Suddenly, I thought of my sterling silverware, one of my prized possessions. Two pieces had mysteriously disappeared from our eight place settings. Everyone in the family knew about the missing pieces, but no explanations were offered. That day, in the center of the circle, I questioned my son about the two pieces of silverware. Tears welled up in his eyes, and he looked toward the floor. His reaction answered my question, but it was important that he actually verbalize what he had done. The counselors coached him to get it off his chest. Facing me, he confessed he had taken two pieces of the silverware because he could get lots of money for them. He knew I treasured this set, but he had taken it anyway because he needed the money for his habit."

Alli felt such sympathy for this courageous woman and her family. "Claudia, didn't you feel angry and betrayed at that point?"

"Actually I felt relieved that the mystery was now solved. I didn't get upset or emotional over this confession. When I returned to my seat in the outer circle, the counselors berated me for not getting angry with him, for not telling him of my disappointment, for not insisting that he replace the sterling. Maybe they were saying that I was, in effect, condoning or excusing what he had done because I did not respond with visible anger when he confessed. But, to be honest, my personality would not have allowed me to show anger in such a setting."

"Claudia, weren't you also protecting your child? Knowing you, I'm sure you felt that his public confession was enough punishment and that he didn't deserve your wrath as well. Obviously, your emotional attachment to your son wasn't shared by the counselors," offers Celia.

Claudia responds, "In my heart, I might have been trying to convince myself that it could have been worse. We knew of a family whose young son had sold all of his mother's sterling silverware, all twelve place settings. Possibly I was rationalizing that Elliot didn't do as much wrong as this other person. Most mothers want to see the good in their children's behavior, even when that behavior is contemptible."

"And...you may have been subconsciously comparing values...the value of those two pieces of sterling with the value of your son's life...there is no comparison, of course. You may have truly forgiven him, so the sterling didn't seem important," Laura suggests.

"Right. I don't want to put too much emphasis on the silverware, which can be replaced. Although I don't dwell on this episode, it has occurred to me that Judas was willing to betray Jesus for thirty pieces of silver and my son was willing to betray my trust and love by taking my silver and selling it for his addiction. A warped or excessive need for money sometimes drives people to betray another person close to them. Addicts aren't alone in making a god out of money."

"Interesting point. Tell us more about the family week encounter," Alli prods.

"The family week encounter was an experience not soon forgotten. During one of the small group sessions, Julie and her mother were in the middle of the circle, their feelings being scrutinized. We discovered that Julie's mother also was a heavy user of alcohol. The counselors tried to get her into the treatment program. She resisted with a barrage of excuses; she and her friend got disgusted and walked out of family week."

"Did Elliot make it through the entire 28-day program?" Barbara inquired.

"Yes, Elliot completed the treatment and managed to stay away from alcohol for a couple of months. He moved back home and took a job. But he resumed drinking when he began socializing with his cronies from work. He just didn't have enough strength to resist temptation. Soon, he was back to square one."

"Some people have to go through treatment more than once," Kate notes, trying to fathom the obvious disappointment in Claudia's manner.

"I know, sometimes more than twice! After a couple of years, Elliot went through treatment again. This time he entered a local Alcohol Rehabilitation Center for a period of four weeks. He attended AA meetings and seemed able to resist alcohol for awhile. Unfortunately, he couldn't resist beer while socializing with his friends. Driving while drinking was another tragic problem, and he was picked up for DWI.

"Again, while he hid his drinking from Martin and me, we worried every day and every night. My greatest fear was that he would drink, drive, get into an accident, and be injured or kill someone. We prayed each day for God's protection of Elliot. Our prayers were answered. Even though Elliot was arrested for DWI's, he was never involved in an accident. He was sent to the state treatment center for a lengthy stay, four months. Counseling, various types of classes, and job opportunities were available there. He came to grips with his problem and wanted to change his life. And, with that, he gained a positive attitude."

"How is he doing today, Claudia?" asks Elizabeth.

"He's doing very well. Since completing this program, Elliot has gone through a lot of soul searching over why he had let a disease like alcoholism almost ruin his life. He needed to be assured of his parents' love in spite of everything that had gone wrong in his life. So, we sometimes talked on the phone for an hour, helping him to sort out and to cope with mistakes he had made. Counseling has helped him see through his own behavior and come to terms with the behavior of others in his life. He continues with counseling and AA meetings. Being open and upfront about his addiction, he's not afraid to say he is a recovering alcoholic and cannot take a drink. People are more understanding about this problem now."

"You must have been emotionally destitute after years of this. How did your ordeal with Elliot affect your other family members?" Alli asks, as she considers Claudia's unbelievable resilience.

"I'm not aware of any really adverse affects. His brothers certainly wanted to see Elliot recover. So, when he needed to talk, he would call his brothers, collect. I'm not sure how happy they were about these calls in the wee hours of the morning. Realizing how much we worried about Elliot, Eddie and Eric didn't want to burden us with any problems they had. Since they lived in another state, we didn't keep up with them on a day-to-day basis, but our bi-monthly phone calls were always an up-date on the pleasurable part of their lives. I felt better after talking with them."

"Claudia, was there any particularly significant event which seemed to trigger Elliot's troubles?" Laura inquires.

"I'm glad you asked that. The fact that his sister, Stephanie, died on his birthday troubled Elliot for many years, something his father and I didn't realize. Her death on December 4 became the most important event for that day and made Elliot's birth on December 4 seem less significant to him by comparison. We always celebrated his birthday, but we couldn't overlook the fact that it was also an anniversary of Stephanie's death. People told me that when Elliot drank, he would talk about his sister dying on his birthday. It took several years before he could tell me that this was disturbing to him. That may have been the catalyst you asked about, Laura. I'm also aware that an alcoholic can and will blame his drinking on anything but himself. Maybe this is Elliot's cop-out."

"Did you ever go to meetings of Al-Anon?" asks Barbara.

"No, we never did. During family week, we said we would go. But when Elliot moved back home and wasn't drinking, it didn't seem necessary. Unfortunately, the thought of sharing this shame with others, even Al-Anon people, wasn't something I wanted to do."

Alli speaks up, "Stories like these are difficult to talk about, but it does help to know that other people have experienced what you have gone through. I, for one, am so grateful to you—and to Elliot—for sharing this experience. I know you asked Elliot's permission to talk about this."

Then, looking at Barbara, Alli says, "Your family member has also agreed to your sharing a difficult period in your lives. I find you generous and caring people to talk about your tough times. You have an Al-Anon story to share, Barbara." As Alli surveys this petite, brown-haired lady, she decides the aging process must have put her on 'hold.' Barbara's short bobbed hair, along with the stylish sports clothes and a friendly smile, seemed to cut twenty years off her age. Alli again marvels at the strength of these women in the face of tribulation. Indeed, God's loving arm has surrounded them.

Help Through Al-Anon.

"Yes, I do want to talk about Al-Anon. Al-Anon has been a tremendous blessing to me," begins Barbara, "and it has truly been an education, too.

"Alcohol controlled our family for many years before we realized what was happening. My husband, John, is a recovering alcoholic. One of the pamphlets I read says that the family will not admit that a member is an alcoholic until the illness has been critical for an average of seven years, and once admitted, the family waits another two years before seeking competent help.

"At first it was just a problem when we attended a party; I would come home furious with John for drinking too much. Soon, I didn't want to go out anymore, so our social life became more and more constricted.

"Next came his car accidents and blackouts. Bracing myself for when John came home late for a meal, I always felt that my job was to control what was going on, to protect, to cover up. This caused tremendous tension in our family. At the supper table I somehow covered up for his words and actions. I was so preoccupied with how to handle John, I wasn't helping the children. In fact, I preferred that they didn't talk to me. My mind was busy thinking of ways to control John's drinking.

"Several times I threatened to leave John. After one of my threats, he assured me that I wouldn't be able to support the children if I did leave. So I was challenged to show him I could. Having been a substitute teacher for a long time, I took a regular part-time teaching job, but soon realized that, indeed, I could not support the kids on this salary. Taking this part-time teaching job required me to take classes to renew my teaching certificate. The Human Relations curriculum included classes on alcoholism where recovering alcoholics spoke to us. My eyes began to open. Could I ever identify with things these alcoholics said!

"Chuck, a friend from John's work, came to talk to me about what was going on. John was leaving work at four o'clock most days to go have a drink, so Chuck suggested that perhaps I should come down town to have coffee with John about that time of the afternoon. Chuck meant well, but it just didn't work that easily.

"The drinking continued. Family tension continued. One day while we waited for John, wondering where he was, I lost my temper with my daughter. She said something I didn't like, and I slapped her face. Quietly she said to me, 'You just can't help yourself can you, Mom?' Then I knew I had to do something. I knew *I* needed help."

"It must have been at this point you started attending Al-Anon meetings," says Claudia.

Nodding, Barbara continues, "Our pastor announced in church that AA had open meetings which anyone could attend. The Lord was leading me to the help I needed. Attending a few AA meetings first, I then went to Al-Anon. In the beginning it seemed necessary to explain at every meeting that I really didn't know if John was an alcoholic. It was helpful just being there, talking about my problems and learning that other people had similar chaos in their lives.

"One lesson I learned was that Al-Anon would not provide me with a solution to John's drinking problem. Rather, they teach a person to work on themselves, to do something constructive with their own lives so that they can be helpful to others.

"John didn't like the idea of my going to Al-Anon, but then he noticed a change in my attitude. Coming to the realization that I was powerless over alcohol and that I could not change the alcoholic in our family, I now understood the first step in the Al-Anon program. Then I began detaching. The children and I ate when planned, whether John was there or not. We went out when and where we planned, whether he was with us or not. Learning that I was unable to control him eliminated the need to scheme and plan, leaving me with much more time for the children and myself."

"What an eye opener, Barbara," Audrey comments.

Barbara adds, "Another step in the Al-Anon program is to turn your will and life over to God, as you understand Him."

Let Go and Let God

"Lying in a hospital bed I did this. During these trying times, I was hospitalized twice for cancer surgery. Unable to help myself or others, unable to control my husband or my children, I asked the Lord to take control. These crises became a blessing, too."

"You know, so few of us knew you were going through so much pain and heartache. I wish we had known and been there for you," Laura says softly. "At least we could have started a prayer chain for you, years ago!"

"Yes. That would've been such a help! We could have used the Round Robin for our prayer requests. Except that, for so long, I was too ashamed to let the rest of you know what was going on. Anyway…the slogan *'Let Go and Let God'* became my reminder. Although I always prayed that the Lord would be with me, I wanted to do things my way. Lying in bed at night, I prayed to God to take care of John and to bring him home safely. But after saying 'Amen,' I'd put my coat on over my nightgown and drive around for hours looking for him. The night of John's first accident I was doing just that—curlers in my hair, a raincoat over my pajamas—never thinking that anyone would see me. Friends had to drive around looking for *me* to tell me John was in the hospital.

"My communication with God was like talking to Him on the telephone, but never putting the phone to my ear, only to my mouth. Another slogan I think of is *'If you worry, why pray? If you pray, why worry?'* Our pastor once made the comparison that the harder you press on the crutches, the more support you get. In the same way, the harder you lean on God, the more strength you get."

"We all have much to learn from your experience, Barbara. What else did you learn from Al-Anon?" asks Alli, adding that she has a couple of friends who may be alcoholics.

Barbara answers, "Another step in the Al-Anon program is to make a searching and fearless moral inventory of ourselves. This is great, but sometimes I don't like what I see. Realizing that alcoholism is a disease was a necessary step in preventing me from being bitter. You see, I thought John drank to hurt me or because of something I did or didn't do. Keeping the disease aspect in mind, I gradually got over my anger."

"What was the turning point?" Alli raises her eyebrows looking at this attractive, freckled-faced woman.

"We both learned to rely on God! With our church's prayer support and help from our pastor, AA, and Al-Anon friends, John and I went to a counselor. This was the turning point.

"Living one day at a time is still important, even after many years of sobriety. We are growing together emotionally and spiritually, living in a relaxed atmosphere, attending events together. There is laughter in our lives now. Although we share our problems, communication is something we are still working on. Al-Anon has been a blessing for us, because it brought us to depend on God for our struggle with John's alcoholism. God doesn't promise to keep us out of trouble, but He does promise to be with us when we are in trouble and to give us the strength we need when we seek it. I've learned to apply Al-Anon steps to other difficult situations as well."

"Barbara, I will always remember your godly Odyssey. Do I understand correctly that when John was recovering, both of you attended Al-Anon and AA open meetings in nearby towns to share this testimony?" Alli asks.

"Yes. We did that for a while in the late 1970s. Now there have been so many years of sobriety that people no longer associate John with alcoholism."

When Barbara concludes her Al-Anon story, Alli clears her throat and hesitates briefly before confessing, "You have changed my perspective. Before hearing you women talk about the alcoholics in your family, I had never thought about them being someone's husband, or father, or son. An alcoholic caused the accident that killed my mother. I become angry when my friends drink to excess, and I won't drink myself. The disease aspect of alcoholism didn't really mean anything to me until now. This has been a learning experience for me."

Rebellious Teenagers

After hearing both alcoholism stories, the group becomes pensive. Alli expresses her appreciation of our willingness to talk about the "warts" in our lives. "Christians are obviously not exempt from problems, but we have an advantage in not only knowing where to go for help, but for lifting our sights to see things in clearer perspective. Sarah, you noted that your family had an awful time with your rebellious teenager."

Alli looks down at the 1956 yearbook picture and once again is taken back by the still-youthful appearance of another Blue Garter Club member. Sarah begins, "My account of teenage rebellion has a happy ending, but not before we were to the brink of despair over what would happen to our son. My first recollection of Kyle's rebellious behavior was the Long-Hair issue when he was in junior high. Jonathan wanted to cut Kyle's wild and frizzy hair. Kyle absolutely refused and stormed out of the house, staying away for quite awhile. Kyle's achievements in sports captured our attention, but we certainly had our heads in the sand regarding the other activities going on in his life.

"Kyle wrote his own account of those rebellious years and the dramatic change in his life shortly before graduation from high school. He said I could read his account to you."

"I am a 34-year-old born-again Christian. In 1976, just before high school graduation, God reached into my heart and made me His own. Living in a suburb of Minneapolis, my life style was similar to that of many other teenagers attending the same school. Although active in sports, many of the students were also involved with drugs, alcohol, and sex. I was no exception.

"Peer pressure was probably the reason I got involved. My parents certainly didn't teach me those things; they don't drink, smoke, or do drugs. Nevertheless, I was strongly influenced by these activities; they were prevalent in my life for reasons I can't explain. By my junior and senior years in high school, I was smoking dope on a daily basis and drinking alcohol on the weekends. Having girlfriends, I became involved in sex as well. Knowing it was wrong did not halt the activity. At least not for awhile.

"Finally, I began to 'want out.' It occurred to me that my performance in various activities, including sports, would improve if I quit smoking dope. Being free of drugs and alcohol became a strong desire, but I didn't know how to change. While I was in this 'hungering for change' mode, I met a man who had experienced the power of God intervening in his life and changing him.

"One evening in May I saw this man, but my instincts were to avoid him, so I did. Later on I saw him again. This time I talked to him, and he wanted to talk to me about God. His timing was right. He caught me when my desire to be free of drugs and alcohol was at its peak, and now I was ready to listen. He told me God could change my life in an instant if I accepted Him as my Lord and Saviour.

"After an hour of talking, he coaxed me into saying a simple prayer in my own words, dedicating my life to God. Now we were Christian brothers, he told me. When I went home I said, 'Mom, I have just done the most amazing thing. I have just made Jesus Christ the Lord of my life.'

"The change was immediate. Although I looked the same—my hair hadn't changed color and I didn't grow taller—I was aware that something inside me had changed. In school the next day the changed feeling was apparent to others. During a free period, my friend wanted me to go with him to smoke dope, but I was able to shun the temptation and say, 'No, I'm not going to do it today.' The next night, a Saturday night, we were having our usual weekend party to smoke dope and drink. I went to the party. Stepping out of my car, an old football buddy, came over to me and said, 'What is it with you? You are different!' I told him about the simple little prayer asking God to get me free of drugs and alcohol and change my life. By now barely 48 hours had passed since I said that prayer and already God had changed me in such a dramatic way it was obvious to other people.

"God became very real to me, which prompted me to pray and read the Bible. Some of my friends also found the Lord through my witnessing. I found new Christian friends. The only old friends I kept were my new brothers in Christ.

"Although I didn't fully comprehend what had happened to me, I knew it was marvelous to have God directing my life. All aspects of my life were affected. I began hearing the phrase 'born again' and soon realized that my experience was this new birth. My old spirit was gone, and I now had a new spirit born of God as recorded in John 3. Since then, I have been a born-again Christian."

Sarah looks up from the paper she is holding and comments on some of the dramatic changes that took place. "He destroyed his record collection; he rarely watched TV; he began attending Bible studies and worship services; he read his Bible and prayed. He joined a Pentecostal non-denominational church. It was certainly the answer to my desperate prayer earlier that year, 'Oh, God, what will happen to Kyle? Please save him.'"

Alli looks around the group, seeing empathy in these faces. "Thanks, Sarah. It's so heartbreaking for parents to see their children involved in behaviors which will eventually destroy them. And…to try to deal with the rebellion. We certainly realize how dependent we are on our Lord, who can work His ways even when we despair that we cannot."

Sarah comments, "Alli, you show maturity beyond your years, even in understanding parental heartbreak."

Claudia adds, "It's apparent that Lutheranism's reticence and formality didn't meet Kyle's needs for spontaneity and repentance as a born-again Christian. Not all Christians have such a dramatic experience. Many of us go along at an even pace throughout life, never leaving the church or forsaking Christ. For us, born-again experience is a daily dying-and-rising in Christ. We are 'born again' every day into God's love and forgiveness. It's probably not as dramatic as what Kyle experienced, but it is a genuine and sustaining rebirth."

Alli turns to her new friend, Mother Earth. "Kate, I noticed your family picture includes a son who sports long hair and earrings. However, a lot depends on the person's rationale for a specific image, doesn't it?"

This, too, shall pass....

Kate responds. "You must be referring to our son, Pierce, the musician. Sometimes he wears his hair long in the middle with the rest of his head shaved. He also wears earrings and even has an earring in his nose.

"Yes, I'd prefer that he had a subdued collegiate haircut like his brothers, but as lead singer with a heavy metal band, he feels he needs to have this unique look. Managing a music store is his primary work.

"His dad grew up in the crew-cut era, so he had a hard time accepting Pierce's strange hair style, but their biggest disagreement was over the earrings. Although Dan and Pierce could never agree on the earrings, they did compromise. Pierce wouldn't wear those earrings to church. On the day of Dan's funeral, I noticed that Pierce didn't wear earrings. Saying, 'I knew Dad wouldn't have wanted me to wear earrings,' Pierce displayed the thoughtfulness we've tried to instill in our children. Keeping open the lines of communication between parent and child is one of the most important aspects of parenting. Don't get bogged down in something as silly as hair and earrings that can result in damaged lines of communication.

"If you don't like your child's grooming style, keep in mind that long hair, earrings, and nose rings are usually harmless identity fads or rebellion. Give your children enough individual attention so you really know them. It's true that gang membership requires some unique look, so you don't want to be naive about what's going on. I wonder if the crew cut was considered pretty extreme 40 years ago? I feel: 'This, too, shall pass!'"

Alli smiles. "Let's break before we talk about another area of family life...disagreements and agreements."

7

Family Life...Disagreements
...and Agreements

Whose Fault

My fault
your fault
stop blaming
start forgiving.

Create love
destroy love
my fault
your fault

Who are you to say
who is to blame.

My fault
your fault

Our fault
our error
our forgiveness

Divine.

© Daphne Lewis

Back again in our circle, we resume our conversation about trying times. Alli has collated our informal essay segments and has highlighted several parental heart-aches. To keep the atmosphere from becoming too somber, she asks, "Do we still have a couple of 'warts' to talk about?" Sighs and nodding heads prompt her to press ahead.

Living Together

"Many of my contemporaries decide to live together without getting married—I suppose you ladies might call it cohabitation or 'playing house.' I doubt this life style meets with parental approval. Some may go along with it, hoping the couple eventually will get married. What exactly is it about living together without marriage that bothers you the most?"

Alli raises her eyebrows in an expectant look. No doubt *all* these women have opinions on this topic.

Sarah volunteers first. "They are missing out on God's best! In one way, the Bible is our instruction manual for living. When purchasing appliances, cars, computers, whatever, we always receive an instruction manual. Our purchased item works much better when we follow the manual; if we refuse to use it, we can expect a breakdown. When God created us, He also provided an instruction manual—the Bible. When we refuse to follow the guidelines of the Bible, breakdowns occur. I'm not suggesting that Christians living by the Bible will have a perfect or trouble-free life, but we can reduce the problems in life when we live by a set of rules designed to benefit us.

"But there's another scriptural side to it. Both Genesis 2 and Matthew 19 say a man shall leave his father and mother, shall cleave to his wife, and the two shall become one. That is a radically different relationship than two Egos making a deal, an uncommitted and temporary arrangement. Cohabitation is such an impoverished view of Male-Female union."

Alli notes a heightened interest in this topic. "I certainly have a lot of friends facing these pressures from their 'significant Other.' Let's keep going!" Sally raises her hand.

"I suppose its sexual aspect is the first thing that comes to mind for our generation, which described this life style as 'living in sin.' Growing up, I was taught that sex is a very sacred union to be shared only within life-long marriage. When excerpts from the now-discredited Kinsey report were published during my teen years, my dad had strong negative opinions about people even talking about sex. He was very out-front about sex being sacred, so we definitely had high values pulling our guidelines. However, we shouldn't be so naive as to think cohabitation is the only life style for 'living in sin,' sexually speaking."

"Many parents have had to face this version of a generation gap with their adult children." Celia's hand shoots up as she begins to speak. "Cohabitation is certainly not something I would condone. On the other hand, a monogamous 'live-in' relationship which is out in the open seems better than a young person prowling through many one-night stands with absolutely no regard for the other person's well-being. We may regard cohabitation as living a lie. But, to my way of thinking, a bigger lie is secretly engaging in the same activities. As parents, we don't accept the cohabitation notion, but we love our children regardless. I can't imagine parents who would disown their children because they were living together outside of marriage."

Our Children in Unhealthy Relationships

Dana volunteers. "Parents get upset at the lack of commitment to a long-term relationship. It's like playing house or pretending to be married, but not really committing oneself to the other person. I guess they figure if it isn't as good as anticipated, one of them can move out. Using this approach, they move in together with an agenda of changing each other into suitable marriage material. All too often, these are nothing less than 'addictive relationships.'"

"What do you mean by that—addictive relationships?" Alli asks.

"Being attracted to people who have abuse problems—such as alcohol—and thinking you can help them overcome their problems. Or, honestly believing you can heal their wounds from some long-past trauma. My daughter used to think she could solve problems for others, but these relationships were rarely healthy."

"I'm sure your heart ached seeing your daughter in an unhealthy relationship. How did you deal with this, Dana?" Alli extends this theme with a personal interest, as she thinks of her present friends.

"Adult children may turn a deaf ear to parental advice at times like this, and they need to learn for themselves. We left the door open for our daughter to come back home when she was ready. I prayed that she'd have the strength to pull away from her codependent relationships and eventually she did, so my prayers were answered. It was a learning experience for me, too.

"I've since learned about other women and men who get caught in abusive relationships and don't have the strength to get out. Many of them have trouble leaving physically and emotionally abusive situations. Marla is extremely tender-hearted, and it took a great deal of strength for her to remove herself from this relationship. I'm very proud of her.

"Who would ever dream that my children's lives would be so complicated. There have been many times I felt like a failure as a mother. But then I realize we live in the 1990s, and today's communities simply aren't the homogeneous little circles I was accustomed to seeing in Minnesota. Alli, your generation has many tough decisions to make." Dana looks weary.

Cohabitation: For Economic Reasons

Citing another rationalization young people use for living together, Alli asks, "Why would parents get upset if young couples live together for economic reasons?"

"Sometimes it may be a matter of fiscal survival," says Kate, our soft-spoken, practical friend, our Mother Earth who has raised a large family. "When our girls moved to New York City to work, Justine, Cloe, and their friend, Joan—along with Justine's fiance—pooled their resources to rent an apartment where all of them lived. That arrangement didn't bother me particularly."

Ann speaks up. "I take exception to the assumption that cohabitation cannot be a loving relationship. My feeling is that many couples who live together do have a loving relationship, but choose not to marry for reasons of their own. Several friends of mine have adult children who dated for many years, got married, and were divorced a year later. I think living together is a way to find out if marriage will work."

Laura interrupts. "That's a common rationale. But research I've seen indicates a 75 percent *failure* rate— much higher than for standard dating patterns—for marriage where the couple lived together before the wedding."

"Maybe a lot of unmarried couples living together do have a loving relationship," starts Renae, "but my sense is that the arrangement breeds a false sense of what marriage is all about. Essentially, moving in or moving out can be done on a whim with no strings attached. This gets back to commitment again. The promises of marriage are missing."

Alli muses: "I notice that many of you are expressing convictions which corroborate with how high a priority you place on Biblical views of marriage." She acknowledges Claudia.

Christian Families Face Illegitimate Births

"One of our greatest parental concerns is for the illegitimate child. This is the second episode in the story of our alcoholic son, so bear with me if it takes a few minutes to tell it." Claudia is getting comfortable in her chair.

"After our son went through one of his alcohol treatment programs, he began dating a woman he worked with and within a few months she was pregnant. There was no intention of getting married; they would rather live together. We certainly didn't approve, but they were adults and our approval wasn't required. Unhappily, we endured their arrangement, hoping they would soon get married. Once again, we went through heartache and indecision.

"This couple had no money, no stable jobs, and no decent place to live. Where does a baby fit into the scheme of things? The father-to-be is an alcoholic. The mother-to-be is a high school dropout, who is a potential alcoholic, codependent on her own mother. With no medical insurance, irregular prenatal visits to the doctor occurred only after payday. What kind of a chance for a fulfilled life did this baby have anyway? Love for this baby was forthcoming, but means to care for it were definitely lacking.

"Nothing about this situation made any sense to either Martin or me. We prayed many prayers on behalf of these young people and their unborn child. Our granddaughter was born prematurely and spent two weeks in an incubator. The mother, for her own reasons, chose to have the birth certificate list the father as 'Unknown.'"

Tears well up in the eyes of the other mothers in this group. "How painful for all of you," Audrey murmurs. Alli shivers as she thinks about the minor problems she inflated and dumped on Claudia; she recalls how patiently Claudia had listened to her and comforted her.

"Since Elliot considered renting a basement apartment that was infested with cockroaches, Martin and I took it upon ourselves to buy them an older mobile home located in a trailer court. Whether or not this was the right thing to do is a question which remains unanswered. As parents we have found it extremely difficult to know when to help our children and when to refuse to help, especially when their need is financial. I so desperately wanted things to improve for them. Yes, I do know about 'enabling' and 'tough love.' I'm sure we were being their enabler."

"Haven't we all been enablers at one time or another?" injects Laura.

Nodding, Claudia continues, "Having an illegitimate grandchild was a terribly shameful thing for me. Our generation expected that babies would not be born out of wedlock. Feeling ashamed, I didn't talk about my grandchild for about a year. In fact, I even lied a couple of times when someone asked if I had any grandchildren. Although I loved this child, the excitement of having my first grandchild was lost because of the circumstances of her birth. Finally, I managed to get over being ashamed, but it was a trying time for me. I felt like a failure as a mother."

"It must have been hard for you to quietly listen while other grandmothers showed pictures and bragged about their grandchildren. What has happened since then?" Alli is curious about Elliot, who is so close to her own age.

"After Elliot's return from his last treatment program, the couple didn't get along. Sylvia decided to move out and, of course, she took our grandchild with her. After a few months, Sylvia married someone else. This new relationship gives us concern for the welfare of our grandchild. Sylvia has also been through treatment for her own alcoholism. Because Elliot's name wasn't on the birth certificate, he is now involved in a court battle to establish paternity and to get visitation rights, which were denied him for several months. Being married would have eliminated many of these problems.

"Our granddaughter is in first grade now, but she has had an education beyond her six years. She has witnessed adults getting drunk, arguing, fighting. We are terribly concerned about what kind of values will be instilled in her as she grows up. It is my hope and prayer that she will be allowed to visit us during summer vacations so that we can get to know her better, be a part of her life and even have a loving relationship.

"Right now I'm feeling drained from recalling all these problems. It's somebody else's turn!!"

Does Living Together Before Marriage Prevent Divorce?

Alli picks up the cue. She can't help wondering what keeps this mother going. "Thanks, Claudia. You've shown us how cohabitation can lead to unhealthy and divisive situations. Are there any more thoughts about this?"

Kate leans forward, looks at the group to see if anyone else is ready to talk. The others seem relaxed and ready to listen, so she begins. "As parents, we know what many of the consequences of cohabitation are, or could be, and we don't want our children to have to suffer those consequences. We are protective of our children. But sometimes, this can also be a lesson they learn the hard way. One of our daughters fell in love with a fellow who moved to Colorado. She went to visit him, not telling us that she had quit her job and intended to stay there. Dan wept when he learned that she planned to stay, but after a couple of months she was back home, having discovered what a jerk this fellow was. I suppose this is exactly the argument our children use. 'Mom and Dad, our living together is one way to find out if we really want to marry this person. Our living together before marriage will lower our chances of a divorce.' According to articles I have read, however, statistics bear out Laura's earlier comment. Divorce is more likely among couples who live together before marriage than it is for couples who marry but have never lived together. If lifelong marriage is the goal, living together before marriage doesn't make divorce less likely."

Glancing around the circle, and with a sweeping gesture, she gives her opinion: "All we have to do is look at our own group. None of us lived together before marriage, but we have all had long-lasting marriages."

Kate continues, "A unique twist to this living arrangement happened in our family when one of our sons became engaged. He asked us if his fiancee could move in with us because her parents were moving, and she was left to find her own housing while going to college. He was willing to give up his room and bunk with his brother. It worked out well for our family. For economic reasons, this type of living arrangement is more prevalent than we might expect. Our future daughter-in-law was a delight and tremendous help during the year Dan was ill. Sterling and I are both so thankful Dan and Megan got to know each other before Dan died."

Alli looks around the group for more input, inquiring, "Isn't the marriage certificate just a piece of paper?"

"Thank God for that piece of paper!" starts Sarah. "It's a legal document necessary for buying and selling property, for medical benefits, and for many other transactions of life. Our feelings can bounce all over the place and be undependable, but that marriage certificate is binding and keeps home a stability zone during times when we may not 'feel' very married. Our marriage may be unraveling, but that marriage certificate holds us together—if only by a thread."

"You feel strongly about that topic!" adds Alli with an uncomfortable laugh.

"Yes I do. I mentioned it earlier: Our marriage almost fell apart at one point, and I'm thankful we had a marriage certificate to prove there was a commitment there somehow. We picked up the pieces and our marriage is now far stronger than ever. You might say the marriage certificate was the 'objective glue' that kept us together until we got our act together."

"The voice of experience. Amen." Audrey agrees.

Families after Divorce: Step-families

Alli looks at Dana and says, "Let's go on with other concerns. Dana, you mentioned your son's divorce and how your grandchild is now part of another family."

Dana says, "Like Claudia, I have a granddaughter who is part of another family. Divorce is excruciating for grandparents, too. Kevin was young and still in college when he was married. He felt he needed to better support his family, so he joined the Army.

"Unfortunately, the marriage didn't survive their European separation, and it ended in divorce. He has tried to re-establish a relationship with his daughter. In some ways this has been easier on her because no tug of war for visitation and care is involved, which I see in other families. However, I know Andrea must have many questions as she gets older.

"There is an up side though! I thank God every day for my own good relationship with Andrea and her family. Andrea lives with her mother, stepfather and their children. Her mother and I have remained friends, and my granddaughter certainly has a good home. Nevertheless, it feels strange to have your own grandchild as part of someone else's family."

"Has your son also remarried?" inquires Alli.

"Yes. While in Europe, he married a widow with a son, so now I have a step-grandchild. Kevin was able to take advantage of the opportunity offered through the military to complete college. He earned both a bachelor's and a master's degree.

"And, our Marla is married to a young man who has an adorable little boy. They are centering their home life in the love of Jesus Christ, which pleases me more than I can say. I have discovered that it isn't at all hard to love and be proud of step-grandchildren."

"Divorce and remarriage makes extended families so complex," says Audrey.

"True. But it also gives me a chance to open my heart, and it gives me more children to love and hug! Isn't that what grandmas are all about?" Dana laughs.

A Unique Oneness in Marriage

Alli glances around the group and gestures toward Laura. "You have written a Bible study on Christian relationships that has become quite influential for tens of thousands of Christians. Could you summarize its basic insights on what constitutes a Christian marriage?"

"Christian marriage brings two individuals into a unique relationship through creation of One New Person," responds Laura. "The Bible tells us that God created Eve as a helpmate for Adam '...the two became one' which we now know refers to such a one new person marriage. Likewise Ephesians 5:31 says, '*For this reason a man shall leave his father and mother and be joined to his wife, and the two shall become one.*' [RSV—note the similar statement in 2:14-16.] The Bible emphasizes the unique oneness of marriage, that a unique new being is created by God at our marriage service. It's as if He brings together two dimes and, from them, creates a quarter."

"Thanks, Laura. That scriptural view underscores why many of us are opposed to 'living together' arrangements," Alli says. "I understand my contemporaries' rationale for living together. But now I've heard the practical and legitimate concerns of parents."

Disagreements With "The System"

Alli says, "Let's move on to discuss another kind of experience. I have several friends who specialize in teaching learning disabled children. Marilyn, you have raised a learning disabled child who also encountered racism in school." Alli again calls upon this strong-willed woman.

Our Son: A Learning Disabled Multi-Race Child

Marilyn explains, "Raising a child with a learning disability can be a very perplexing experience for parents. Many times I have been thankful that Jeffrey was our fourth child because we had personal experience with child development by that time. When Jeff was four, we realized he had a handicap. Knowledge of learning disabilities wasn't widespread. We were certainly unaware of this area in special education, although it was beginning to unfold. We did know that a learning disabled child is not retarded.

"As a kindergarten teacher, I knew that pre-schoolers are eager to learn to write their names. Jeff, however, could not physically write. We took him to a pre-school screening program that identified some lag in small motor skill development. Unfortunately, there was no follow up. In kindergarten he was finally able to write J-E-F-F, but it was difficult for him. He was tested again and once more his small motor skill development was deficient. As parents we felt he should be retained in kindergarten, but the school wanted him to go on to first grade, in special education. Hindsight tells me our parental instincts were accurate; he wasn't ready for first grade.

"Jeff was also hyperactive or possibly suffered from attention deficit disorder. For five years he took the drug, Retalin, which helps to keep a hyperactive child calmed down. Because it's a mind-altering drug, it is available only by prescription. We didn't want Jeff to have this crutch throughout his life, so he knew he wouldn't take it forever."

"Is his learning disability in one particular area?" asks Audrey.

"It seems to be most prevalent in writing; math and science are also difficult for him. During elementary school he was in a regular classroom, but he would go to special education classes in math and language arts. He stayed with his regular class for science and managed to get through it with difficulty. Falling farther and farther behind, Jeff was tested through the school system several times. Finally, we decided to have him tested at an independent agency. They couldn't determine if he was literate. Jeff was ready to enter fourth grade and the school said he should be retained. This time, Jerome and I were opposed to holding him back; we felt this would be detrimental to Jeff at that time of his life. Parents of special education children have a certain amount of

clout because federal funding supports these programs.
The school listened to us.

"His reading ability seemed to take great strides
during fourth grade. Something clicked for Jeff at this
stage in his development. By the time he graduated
from high school, he was reading at the eleventh grade
level."

"That's good! A lot of high school graduates can't
read at that level!" exclaims Alli.

"His oral contributions in class were quite impressive, but when it was time for a test he couldn't pull his
thoughts together and write them down. Writing remains one of his greatest disabilities."

"Will he ever go to college or a technical school?"
asks Elizabeth.

"At this point, we don't know. Right now he's not
ready for college. He has a job for the first time in his life,
and it's providing him some maturation. We didn't
allow him to work in high school because his greatest
need was to gain a basic academic education."

"What about extracurricular activities? Did he take
part?" asks Dana, who continues to be so interested in
music. "Coming from a musical family, he must sing or
play an instrument."

"Yes, he plays the double bass and is very good at it.
Actually, he could have had a music scholarship to
college. However, if you can't handle the academic part
of college, there is really no point in going. Some colleges, including Concordia, have programs to assist
students with learning disabilities. With that assistance,
he could function on the college level. These programs
are very costly and have few students, but as his parents, we would be thrilled to have him graduate from
Concordia like the rest of the family."

"Marilyn, tell about your experience with racism
toward Jeff." Alli surveys her notes as she speaks.

When Racism Rears Its Ugly Head—

Marilyn continues, "Bringing a multi-race baby home to Missoula wasn't a problem. Jeff was really born into his peer group there; he was accepted because we were accepted. We probably lived in the right place for raising a multi-race child. Nevertheless, every school year some racial incident caused him heartache. Coming home from school with a sad face one day, he told me a little girl wouldn't hold his hand because it was black.

"Moving to Denver when Jeff was in eighth grade exposed him to the ugliness of racism which he could not understand, nor could we. Because we have raised Jeff to be proud of who he is, his first encounter with racism in school caused a ruckus. Walking in the hallway one day early in the school year, a white male student came up to him and said, 'Nigger, bow down to me!' Jeff answered, 'No way' and slammed this kid against the wall, bumping his head. The next day, the principal called him into the office. After explaining to the principal exactly what had happened, Jeff was told, 'If you have to do that again, do it away from school.' The principal didn't want to deal with it. I felt a better solution would have been to bring the two young boys face to face to talk about their encounter and about their need to get along regardless of skin color."

"The Denver public schools are quite racially mixed," Elizabeth adds. "Did he find a peer group to identify with?"

"He did in high school. But our first year in Denver was really a hard one for him. Because he was black, many of the white kids wanted nothing to do with him. But one group started getting friendly, and Jeff thought he found friends. Wanting to become part of this group, he asked for a jean jacket with a certain patch, which we gladly bought for him. Not until we went to school for a parent-teacher conference did we learn that his new-found friends were part of a gang and the jean jacket and patch were their symbol. One of the teachers, who is a member of our church, told us she was concerned about Jeff associating with this gang during school. As new-comers to this metropolitan area, we were totally igno-rant of gang activity and so was Jeff. After that parent-teacher conference, we sat down with Jeff, explaining everything the teachers had told us. He was in tears, but understood the need to curb this friendship. For the remainder of his eighth-grade year, he was an outsider who watched from the sidelines. He really had no friends."

"The picture changed when he entered high school, right?" Alli asks hopefully.

"Yes, he went to a different school where there were many more black and Hispanic students, and he found good friends there. It is interesting to me that of the three cultures in his biological background, he has chosen the black culture for historical identity. While living in Montana, we had abundant opportunities to expose him to the Native American portion of his heritage. We did this through books and cultural events. Living in Denver, we have attended various cultural activities of Spanish origin, such as Cinco de Mayo. And we also try to observe the Juneteenth celebration. We want him to know and appreciate his rich cultural mixture."

"What is Juneteenth?" asks Sally.

"Juneteenth is the name given to celebrating June 19, 1865, the day the news of the Emancipation Proclama-tion of 1863 reached Texas. It has become a day of celebration across the Southwest, a cultural event for blacks as well as other races," Marilyn answers.

"In spite of having such a rich and varied heritage, Jeff is a black person, and I suppose he still encounters racism on a regular basis," Alli suggests.

Marilyn replies, "You are so right. Our other children have no idea what Jeff has had to go through growing up, only because of the color of his skin. A muscular young man, he has to be on guard constantly because his physical presence can intimidate people, even though his manner isn't at all threatening. With present gang problems, police will walk up to him when he's talking to friends on the street and ask him what gang he belongs to; or they will remove his cap to see if there is a gang name inside. When this happens, he has to be very careful how he reacts because a comment or misinterpreted move on his part can trigger some unpleasant response by the police."

"For most of us, racism is something we only hear about or observe from the sidelines, but for you, Marilyn, it is part of your family life," Alli observes. "Tell us about having a foster child in your home." Alli marvels at this caring woman who has reached out to help other people.

A Native American Foster Child

"We had Ila, a Native American, as a foster child during her first grade school year. At that time, Nancy was also in first grade, Debra was in fourth grade, and Tom was a toddler. We were living in Montana near an Indian reservation. Various churches in the area began a program to enrich the educational opportunities for these Indian children. The plan was to place disadvantaged children in foster homes during the school year so they could attend public school. When they went back to the reservation during the summer months, their education could benefit them, their parents and others. Little, if any, money was available for this program, so families willing to take a foster child had to provide clothes, shoes, and other necessities out of their own resources. Participants were criticized by activists for taking foster children into their homes, however. Whether this criticism was justified is not really the issue. As a participant, we viewed the situation as an opportunity—children were not getting an education and our community could do something about it. It seemed like the thing to do. Nothing would get done if people base their decisions about getting involved on whether or not they will be criticized.

"Ila was with us only the one school year and then lived with another family for about five years. Because I was sick so much during the year Ila was with us, we didn't feel we could take her another year. It was necessary for me to get my health and strength back before taking on the responsibility of another child. Having Ila prepared us somewhat for our adoption of Jeff several years into the future. From time to time, Ila visited us; when we adopted Jeff, she came to see him. She asked why we had not adopted her. Explaining that she was not available for adoption did not satisfy her. She failed to understand our need to have a child belong to our family permanently, not on a temporary foster care basis.

"On the reservation, Ila lived with her grandparents and her mother, an unstable woman. She didn't know her father. Sadly, Ila's life didn't turn out well despite living with foster families and attending public school for several years. After dropping out of school, she worked from time to time. She had several children, but when she failed to care for them, they were taken from her by the Indian social services agency. After buying a car, Ila drove without ever having a driver's license. More than her car disappeared when her live-in boyfriend left town. Later, another live-in boyfriend stabbed her, and she came to us for help. While she stayed with us, we helped her get a GED. We tried to help her get a driver's license and tried to enroll her in a nursing program. After six weeks, Ila said she couldn't stand living this way any more and had to hit the road. This meant she would either be riding the rails again or going back to the reservation. In spite of opportunities for a better education, Ila was caught in a clash between two cultures. Our good intentions didn't help her improve her lot in life. We've had no contact with her since that time. This was a sad experience for our whole family."

Alli observes. "I think we can all identify with your feelings of frustration over wanting to help, but seeing that your help is not benefiting its recipient."

Alli glances through her notes. "I'm overwhelmed at the depth of you women. You've taken risks, and you've put your hearts on the line."

Adult Children As Close Friends

Alli's voice cracks as she continues. "Several of you indicated in your written comments that your adult children are your dear friends at this juncture of your life. If my mother was a lot like you women, I just know we would have been best friends."

Barbara responds. "Knowing your mother, Alli, you are absolutely right. She would have treasured your friendship as much as you would have enjoyed hers. Now I hope you'll consider our Blue Garter Club members as your close friends."

Barbara shifts to her own situation. "It isn't always a smooth transition from parenting to friendship roles. When a child is obedient and does what she's told, it's easy for a mother to continue making the decisions and controlling that child much longer than is necessary or appropriate. I was that kind of mother! Our oldest daughter was that kind of child!

"While driving together in the car one day, Jane tried to tell me in a very nice way that she had to make her own decisions. My feelings were so hurt; I cried and cried. My next reaction was total detachment; I didn't even want to help her. Finally, I began to realize that Jane had always taken my advice and followed my suggestions. Now she was in college, and I was continuing to control her! When it dawned on me that she could think for herself, and I could still be there when she wanted an opinion on something, I felt much better. Letting our children grow up is sometimes hard on parents, but grown-up children make wonderful friends."

Dana grins at Barbara. "You took the words right out of my mouth, Barbara. Even though we agonized over our daughter's relationships, the Lord was still at work in her. Now, with all of that trauma behind us, she has turned into a most wonderful daughter: sensitive, loving and caring. Sometimes I think it took the death of her father for her to realize that I was a human being, vulnerable, with real feelings. I was not the authoritative figure *she* had envisioned me. In recent years, we've grown even closer, and I can't ask for a better friend."

"Your expressions tell me that you are in agreement about grown-up children making wonderful friends." Everyone nods as Alli continues. "Sally, you are the one who suffered the most from the empty-nest syndrome."

An Empty-Nest Syndrome

"Yes," Sally said, "I turned into a basket case when our fourth (and last) child was ready to go to college. She is our only daughter, so maybe that had something to do with it. Anyway, the summer before her freshman year at Concordia, she worked at the bank downtown, not very far from the office where I worked. We live in a small town, so every day we went home for lunch.

Since Carolyn didn't have her own car, she relied on me. As summer wore on and thoughts of Carolyn leaving for college raced through my head, my anxiety level was at an all-time high. When I left my office at noon, the tears would start flowing. Since it was only a three-block drive to the bank, I had to compose myself quickly so she wouldn't know I'd been crying. This turned into a daily scene.

"Finally, it was time to take Carolyn to Concordia for her first fall semester. Rolf, our very perceptive oldest son, was aware of the difficult time I was having. From all of the children, he sent a card which I will treasure forever. He wrote on it:

> *I know this is not an easy time for you, but you wouldn't want it any other way, would you? You have a daughter most mothers dream about. Nothing will ever change. You know that. There aren't two people who are better able to handle the adjustment than you two. You should be very proud of what you've done and will keep doing. You will always be Mom and Dad to us."*

Alli was surprised at how mellow this witty lady became when speaking of her adoring children.

"My loneliness was still very real, but it did get a little easier each year when she left for college. When you were talking about adult children making good friends—it was like I was sending away my best friend. And, I think it works in reverse, too. Adult children also consider their parents good friends. This is the same kind of relationship I had with my parents."

Alli notes, "Yes, we remember how you talked about crying for three minutes on the phone when your parents called you at the dorm, Sally."

"I always envied the close and loving relationship you had with your parents, Sally," comes a voice from across the room.

Triumphs Which Make Us Proud

Alli thanks Sally and shifts the focus, "We have spent some time talking about family trials as well as family friendships. In spite of setbacks, you women have raised children who have been very successful. Although you believe that the tribulations you and your children have been through have strengthened your character and reliance on God, success stories are more easily spoken of—going to college, graduate school, seminary, medical school, law school, studying hard for a chosen career. Sounds familiar, doesn't it?

"Blue Garter Club members' children are teachers, nurses, lawyers, artists, musicians, media producers, business entrepreneurs, engineers, financial analysts, students, housewives and mothers. Also among your offspring are a pastor, a medical doctor, a bank manager, an accountant, a computer information analyst, and a golf pro. What diversity among your offspring! At the same time, your values have been 'owned' by most of these children, even those who took a detour on the way to discovering those values. Your children's accomplishments would make any parent proud."

Alli summarizes, "From your questionnaires, I learned that twelve children of Blue Garter Club members graduated from Concordia, and several met their spouses at Concordia. Five of your offspring chose North Dakota State University, and two chose University of North Dakota. Two Blue Garter offspring attended the University of Minnesota and two went to Moorhead State College.

"Georgetown University, Valparaiso University, Texas Lutheran College, St. Olaf, University of Maryland, schools in Indiana, Iowa, Idaho, Arizona, and Wisconsin, as well as several graduate schools are also represented. Your overwhelming commitment to higher education is apparent. Some of your children decided on careers that didn't require a college education, and you've obviously been very supportive of their decisions, too."

Generations

Alli sets aside her notes as she wraps up this session. "I'm impressed that two of you represent three generations of Concordia graduates. Laura's father graduated in the early 1920s, and two of her children graduated from Concordia in the 1980s. Barbara's mother graduated from Concordia, as did Barbara and two of her three children. Tradition...that's a *lot* of tradition!

"Thank you for sharing your family's agreements and .disagreements. After we take a seventh-inning stretch, we'll return to discuss your career choices...and perhaps your lack of choices."

8

Careers...
Choices and Changes

The Decade of the '50s

Women and Careers

If I become a teacher
    Will the classroom be my limit?
Or can I look to future days
    With the title 'Principal' in it?
        —No way! No way!
        It's the decade of the '50s!

If I pursue advanced degrees—
    Will my role in life still be to please
The men around me who run the show
    And won't acknowledge what I really know?
        —You bet! You bet!
        It's the decade of the '50s!

If I want to help make people well—
    In a hospital setting, please do tell
Can I be the doctor? Or is the biggest sell
    Making nurses of the women
    To answer the patient's bell?!
        —Right on! Right on!
        It's the decade of the '50s!

If I take a liking to the field of law...
Would men look at me as though seeing a flaw?
"A woman in the courtroom? Never as a judge!
Maybe she would cry and leave her makeup
in a smudge!"
—Case closed! Case closed!
It's the decade of the '50s!

If I have a yearning to serve my Lord and Master,
But I can't sing...
and my cooking's a disaster,
If I don't sew quilts, and my typing must be faster—
Why won't the seminary make me a lady pastor?
—You're forgiv'n! You're forgiv'n!
It's the decade of the '50s!

If my main desire and goal in life is
to marry Mr. Right
To keep his house and wash his clothes—
from morning until night,
To be a mother, stay at home,
keep children in my sight,
Then, I'm successful!
Don't refer to this as woman's plight!
—Good cookin'! Good cookin'!
It's the decade of the '50s!

HOWEVER...HOWEVER...HOWEVER

Now I've lived through those days of yore—
And ventured where women did not venture before,
I've taught the kids, nursed the sick, and
typed letters galore.
But, I realized the demands on me
required producing more!
—Keep going! Keep going!
It's the decade of the '60s!

Women in the '50s were not part of women's lib—
But yet we blazed a trail for baby girls still in the crib.
 We didn't burn our bras
 Or march the streets arm-in-arm.
Instead, we quietly prepared for society's new alarm!
 —Moving on! Moving on!
 It's the decade of the '70s!

Demands were made on women
 to help with paying the bills.
Buy a house! Pay for the car!
 We already live without frills.
Dental braces and college spaces
 make parents need headache pills,
As inflation clearly stated:
 We need women with multiple skills!
 —Getting there! Getting there!
 It's the decade of the '80s!

Women are more involved now—
 It's just part of life's new game
Doctors, lawyers, engineers—
 It's definitely not the same
As the decade of the '50s
 when women could never claim
A place in corporate offices,
 where men still seek their fame!
 —Hang On! Hang On!
 It's the decade of the '90s!

© Carol Wade Lee

Alli laughs and says, "You all need to know that I heard this poem set to 'rap' and performed at a Mother-Daughter Banquet I attended with Claudia. What fun! It was great! Now it's time for you to talk about yourselves and your own accomplishments. Blue Garter Club members certainly didn't permit the social structure of the 1950s to starve self-expression in the work place. Each of you prepared to be a teacher, and with one exception, each of you did teach. Several obtained master's degrees. A variety of vocations are represented among you, including some lengthy teaching careers. Some of you have stayed at home to be domestic engineers.

"Today's society expects people to change careers several times in their lifetimes, in contrast to some years ago, when remaining for a lifetime in the same job was the norm. As a group, you women have exercised all options. Let's take a look at your early work experiences, as well as your present vocations."

Laura

Before the 1950s—

"Okay...Laura, you started working at a young age and haven't quit. Why don't you start on this topic?" Alli gestures toward Laura.

"Yes, I was only 14 when I had my first 40-hour-a-week job. Not unlike girls today, I worked as a waitress from 4 p.m. till midnight. But unlike today's harried waitresses, my weekly pay after deductions was $16.20—50 cents an hour. When one has gone through a summer earning wages like that, the importance of getting an education is reinforced."

The 1950s—and beyond

Alli nods her head in agreement. "I see from your questionnaire that you earned a master's degree in counseling. Was that helpful to you in the job market, Laura?"

"Yes, it was. But Alli, eat your heart out. In 1956, my teaching contract in a Minneapolis suburb read 'Annual Salary $3,200.' After earning a master's degree in counseling at South Dakota State University, my salary jumped to a spectacular $4,800 in 1958. Was I ever pleased!

"Working full time was not optional for me. While my husband was in graduate school, I taught in four different high schools. Teaching and counseling were both rewarding and fascinating professions; I was a counselor four years in one city and seven years in another. I taught in a Financial Institute in Chicago for five years. When I had our first baby, I taught correspondence courses from my home. Every time a child napped, I worked. I even took my papers to the hospital when my babies were born. Much work was done in the wee hours of the morning."

Alli breaks in, "It sounds as though you have more varied work experience than anyone else in the group, so I want to come back to you."

ᗪ*ana*

The Past—

Alli looks toward vivacious Do-Re-Me. "Dana, you have taught music, owned a business, and worked in other capacities as well. Tell us about that."

"Yes, I loved teaching elementary music both full time and part time. Teaching elementary and junior high groups and ensembles was my special joy, especially when our own children were my music students from third grade on up to junior high. Helping in our insurance business was my least favorite work experience. Later we were in the jewelry business along with my Scandinavian Imports business. This business leaves me with pleasant memories, and I appreciated learning about my own Scandinavian heritage. It didn't take long to learn that I was not a 'born' salesperson like my husband and daughter."

Dana . . . Much later—like now!

"For several years now I have worked in a hospital, first as admitting clerk, and more recently as a secretary in human resources. I have had to hone my typing skills and learn computer data entry. Learning is a constant part of my life. Although my work experience has been varied, music is still my first love. I'm thankful I can participate in music through my church."

Kate

Mother Earth: Then and Now—

Alli motions to Kate. "You have your own business, Kate. How did you get into that?"

"My teaching experience lasted only one year. For most of our married life, I was a full-time housewife, mother of six, and a volunteer. When the children grew up, I needed something more, so I worked with Dan in his insurance business and eventually became an insurance agent. Now that I'm alone, I'm grateful to have my own business and grateful to be working out of my own home."

Job Hunting in the '50s—A Piece of Cake

Sarah

Sarah, a long-time teacher, leans forward. "Let me explain how Jonathan and I landed our first teaching jobs. Today's protocols for job hunting contrast with how informally—even accidentally—we used to go about it. Graduation day was approaching when Jonathan received a call from a school superintendent who was reviewing math major credentials from Jonathan's college. Jonathan was offered a teaching and coaching position by phone—no applications, no interviews. Jonathan explained that he was soon to be married: Was there an opening for a business teacher? 'Yes, can your bride-to-be play the piano?' An affirmative response prompted the superintendent to say, 'Oh good. Then I can kill two birds with one stone.'

"In our next job search, we were driving through a small town and, on a whim, we phoned the school superintendent. He asked if we could come over right away. Wanting to be properly dressed for an interview, Jonathan changed into his suit right there in the car! He signed a contract with that school, and we lived there three good years.

"Later, we tried a few business ventures—buying an apartment building and even a pizza business, but we didn't keep them very long. After staying home for ten years, in the late '60s I went into special education, just when that field was opening up. I became certified in special education by going to night school and summer school. I taught until 1985."

Sarah: In the late '80s and Today

"Since then I have concentrated on volunteer work through our church. While delivering meals on wheels once a week for about five years, I became fond of the senior citizens I met. At the same time, I volunteered in a food and clothing distribution center called PRISM, People Responding in Social Ministry. With citizens' collapsing confidence in the government's ability to solve problems, I suspect our country will have to rely more and more on the voluntary sector to get needs met."

Sally

Sally, The Wit: Then—

Sally nods at Sarah's stories because of similar experiences. "My first teaching job came about because the school system wanted Paul so badly. I took courses required for me to teach elementary music and became part of the deal! So, I never applied, never had to interview.

Sally . . . Much later

"When our children were going to college, I needed to boost our income. I walked into an insurance office and asked if they were looking for office help. The man said, 'Yes. When can you start? Tomorrow will be fine.' No interview! A couple of years later, the same thing happened for my next job: No interview, start tomorrow. When I see our children going through their job-hunting process with applications, resumes, and interviews, it is mind boggling to me. I wouldn't have a clue where to begin."

Claudia

Then, a Teacher—

Claudia interrupts. "Getting my first teaching job required traveling to Nebraska for an interview. Four of us rode with Elizabeth to the Lincoln/Omaha area one weekend so I could be interviewed. Elizabeth always said I got the job because I wore my little white hat! Wearing a red and white checked suit made me look at least somewhat professional. To this day, I can't believe I actually wore a hat on a job interview!" Claudia shakes her head as the group joins in laughter.

"I taught typing, shorthand, and bookkeeping. My first teaching contract was for $3,200 with a $100 bonus for finishing the year. Women teachers considered this the 'pregnancy clause.' After three years, I resigned my teaching position so we could start a family. It was always my intention to go back to teaching."

Claudia . . . Much Later

"In the 14 years I was a full-time mother, however, the field of office automation advanced in technology and the big explosion was just around the corner. Memory typewriters, word processors, and computers appeared in offices. Mimeograph and Ditto machines were added to the relic heap. With my typing teacher background, my later work often involved specialized typing assignments—forms, programs, reports, certificates, booklets. It was fun! I became a perpetual college student. I'm interested in technological changes in office automation, so I continue with studies and work in computer, word processing, and desk-top publishing, as well as political science and nutrition courses."

Claudia: In the 90s—

"As a legal secretary, I became fascinated with law, so I seized the opportunity to go to school to become a legal assistant. Being one of the oldest students in the program (at age 56) didn't bother me, because nobody treated me differently. I wore jeans and tennis shoes and carried a book bag just like the other college students! After fulfilling my dream and obtaining a certificate in legal assisting, I have been unable to get a job! Age discrimination in the workplace is a very real thing, albeit illegal. And, Sally, I've sent out enough application letters and resumes and have had enough interviews for all of us!!"

Alli suggests, "With your skills, it does sound as though you're an object of age discrimination."

Sally perks up with, "Claudia, try wearing your little white hat next time!" The group roars.

Renae

Teaching for Traveling in the '50s

Glancing at Renae, Alli comments, "I'd like to do what you did! You have traveled more than anyone in the group, starting with a summer in Europe after your first year of teaching. How did you manage to save enough money on a teacher's salary?"

"Looking back, I still don't know how I managed that trip in the summer of 1957. I didn't save any money during the school year; instead I borrowed $1,000 from the bank against my summer teaching checks. That covered my round-trip ticket, as well as expenses incurred while in Europe. Relatives provided hospitality for me in Paris, Norway, and England. I traveled by bus throughout Europe. My bank loan was repaid with my summer teaching checks. It's hard to believe I spent three months in Europe for only $1,000, including travel. Times have changed, haven't they, Alli?"

"Sure have! Did you travel alone?" asks Alli.

"Yes, the first time I was alone. In the summer of 1959, I went back again, traveling with a teacher friend. A daily diary of events, hotels, and costs provides interesting reading 33 years later! We visited relatives and traveled by Eurail pass for two full months. I remember buying a Norwegian sweater for $14.20; today they sell for $200."

Alli interjects, "You not only traveled a lot, but you taught in several states, too, didn't you?"

Renae . . . Later

"I taught in three different schools in Minnesota. Then I decided to go to summer school at the University of Hawaii. I stopped in Denver to visit Elizabeth and applied to teach there. After two years in Denver, Jerry and I were married, and the military life began for me. Now I *really* had a chance to travel. At our first location in New Mexico, I taught full time. Later I was a substitute teacher in military high schools in Wiesbaden (Germany) and Mississippi."

Renae . . . Now

"And now my work in an import shop fits in well with my home economics background, my love of travel, and learning the cultures and customs of other countries."

ʘarbara

A Widespread Career in the 1950s

"Barbara," Alli looks up from her notes, "your career has been widespread."

Barbara responds. "Right! Widespread in the sense that my first year of teaching was in Minnesota, 30 miles from the Canadian border, and my second year was in California, 30 miles from the Mexican border! It was also widespread in terms of community expectations for schools. Family living units in the home economics curriculum in Minnesota evoked a lot of criticism. While in southern California, one of my extra duties was to supervise the girls' bathrooms to catch anyone smoking. Even back then, the girls chit-chatted freely about sex and pregnancy. Substitute teaching keeps me in touch with what's going on in education and in teenagers' minds."

Elizabeth

The Artist: Then and Now—

Glancing to her left, Alli asks, "Elizabeth, tell us how you got into teaching elementary and junior high art."

"It's what I do best, and after 22 years it's hard to imagine doing anything else. I took a few years off to start a family, but I returned to the classroom when our youngest of four children was in kindergarten."

Alli interrupts. "Why did you choose art?"

"When I registered at Concordia, I planned to be a history teacher. It was discouraging to hear: 'The coach is always the history teacher. You will never get a job.' So, I started in home economics. After six weeks of white sauces, I knew I had to find another major, so I transferred into elementary education and art education.

"Art might be specialized, but it can be incorporated into different curriculum areas. One way we learn about other cultures and civilizations is through their art, since it was central to their daily living. For instance, this is the 500th anniversary of Columbus' discovery of America. My older students have already done wonderful sculptures in pre-Colombian style and, later on, all of my students will be learning aspects of pre-Colombian art. My interest in history is brought to life in this kind of art teaching."

"What changes have you teachers observed over those years in public school systems?" wonders Alli, knowing these changes will affect her.

From a Teacher's Perspective

"The demise of the family and battered children are the biggest problems the schools are seeing, in my opinion," says Elizabeth. "The number of children coming from abusive situations is truly shocking. Granted, I teach in an urban area, but I'm guessing that half of my students come from dysfunctional homes. As youngsters, we probably all had a spanking, but there is a radical difference between a spanking and the abuse these kids are getting."

Alli inquires, "Elizabeth, from a teacher's perspective, how do you account for the increase in child abuse?"

"There is enormous pressure on today's families. Inflation—two careers—just survival in some cases! Many parents haven't bothered to learn parenting skills. Their values systems have collapsed to selfish levels and, with that, they've lost perspective on what's worth getting upset about. Many parents don't want the schools to teach values and morals, but far too many parents neglect doing the job themselves. They don't demonstrate a healthy values system in the way they treat their kids."

"Aside from visible bruises, how do teachers sense that a child is abused?" asks Alli.

"One clue that a child is having serious problems is that he or she does not want to be touched. The child may also become very rebellious, because school is the only place where he can be in control of his life. We have a school social worker who works with groups of children having problems. Parenting classes are also offered."

Marilyn relates another insight. "A pupil's behavior quite often alerts school personnel to a potential problem. In one case, we observed the behavior of a little girl on the playground where she would lie down and spread her legs apart while boys circled around her. The state Child Protective Service (CPS) was notified of this behavior and put her through some counseling tests, but she refused to respond. Whether she was a victim herself and had repressed the experience or whether she had witnessed this behavior at home wasn't determined. CPS is continuing their surveillance."

Alli comments, "Schools are legally required to report suspected cases. Elizabeth, how does teaching art help identify abused children or help them overcome the trauma?"

"Children reveal a lot about themselves through their drawings. Art therapy is sometimes used to help troubled children, but that's not my expertise. We can get too analytical and overly suspicious, of course. There is a story about an art teacher who told the school psychologist about a little boy who colored everything black. They were sure he must be very depressed if he didn't see life in full color. Finally they asked the child why he only used black. His answer was perfectly logical: He had lost all of his other crayons!"

"It doesn't sound like you are ready to retire and leave it all behind," comments Dana.

"Not for a couple of years. I enjoy teaching, and I'm committed to helping these youngsters grow through their artistic expression."

"Thanks, Elizabeth." Alli redirects the conversation. "Aimee, your teaching career exceeds 30 years. Tell us about teaching in a high technology area at a vocational school."

Aimee

Teaching Their Grandchildren!

Aimee begins. "I just completed 32 years of teaching—30 of them in the same vocational school. It makes me feel old when I realize I have taught the children of my first students and may soon teach their grandchildren! But I still find teaching enjoyable, partly because of the changing technology in my field of office automation.

"Keeping a step ahead of the students, teachers also learn from them. An exploding field of technology contributes to my interest, but it's exhausting trying to keep up. Textbooks always need updating. In 1979 I earned my master's in education from North Dakota State. Many faculty members coast into retirement for the last five years, but if I was ever so tempted, teaching in this area of constant change wouldn't allow me to do that."

"What kind of changes have you seen in the students over these thirty years?" continues Alli.

"There are many more older students in vocational education who return to school because of a job loss, a divorce, or becoming a single parent. And they bring a whole set of problems with them. Their need for education and retraining often gets narrowly focused because of family responsibilities. Older students are a pleasure to work with, although they are more demanding both of themselves and of their instructors. Wanting to see a practical application for what is being taught, they demand accountability on the part of their instructors, which is not bad! And the maturity they bring to the classroom shows up in their willingness to learn. They've already been out in the real world! It's all quite different from expectations of my public school students."

"Thanks, Aimee," Alli smiles. Let's move on to another teacher. Marilyn, you've been teaching for several years, and, like others here, you earned a master's degree. Let's hear from you."

Marilyn

On the Bench for Twenty Years

"After teaching for three years in either kindergarten or first grade, I took a 'leave of absence' for twenty years to be at home with my children.

"Renewing one's career after such a long recess is very difficult. Education had changed in many areas. Our oldest of four children was in college and our youngest in kindergarten when I resumed my career. My earlier years of teaching had been in North Dakota and Minnesota, but now I had to become certified in Montana. After taking the required classes for certification, I began applying for jobs. When I was invited to become a substitute kindergarten teacher on a half-time basis, I figured this would be a good way to ease back into my career. When a full-time teacher hadn't been found by fall, I was asked to take over the class. I'd been sitting on the bench for twenty years and now I was back in the game! It was a tough year! So many changes!

"The next year I moved to a different school and things began going more smoothly. After six years at this school, I was reluctant to leave this position I loved so much, but we were moving to Colorado. While teaching, I had been taking classes toward a master's degree at the University of Montana.

"Once again I had to be certified. Teacher certification now required a series of tests to ensure competency in all areas of teaching. Since my teaching was on the kindergarten level, I hadn't kept up with the new math. I flunked the mathematics portion of this timed test! Candidates are required to pay a fee to take the tests, so I made sure I was fully prepared for the math portion the second time around. Although I understand the need for assuring teacher competency, this testing procedure made me feel like I had to jump through hoops to get a bone."

"So...did you get the bone?" asks Dana.

"Eventually. But after getting my Colorado teaching certificate, I was disappointed with the bleak job market. So at age 54, I obtained a master's degree in early childhood education from the University of Colorado, Denver."

You cost too much...how old are you?

"Having a master's degree must have made it much easier to get a teaching job," interjects Alli.

Marilyn quickly responds. "Alli, as much as I hate to say this, my master's degree did not help me get a job in the public schools. Strapped for funds, the schools are looking for the least expensive educators. My master's degree put me into a higher salary range. Since I had been subbing, my abilities were well known. Even this didn't provide me with an 'in.' There are so many applicants for every position, it's difficult to even get to the interview stage. And, I think age discrimination was part of it. Although it's illegal to ask a person's age on an application, it's easy to figure out an applicant's approximate age." Pointing to her gray hair Marilyn adds, "Here's another tell-tale sign!"

"Since you eventually got the 'bone,' we know your persistence paid off," says Claudia. "Maybe I need to hear more about your persistence."

Doors open...and close...and open...

Marilyn continues. "When one door closes, another door opens. I began looking at private schools. While attending an education fair, I talked with an assistant from the Denver Archdiocese about an inner-city Catholic school. This parochial school serves a 95 percent Hispanic population.

"'Would you hire someone like me?,' I asked this archdiocese assistant. 'I'm a Lutheran; in fact, my husband is a Lutheran pastor.'

"She said, 'No problem! You don't have to be Catholic to teach in our schools.' She took my name and other information.

"I was called to teach music. The schools were desperate for music teachers. Although I had a minor in music, I didn't want to teach music, partly because it requires a constant high-energy level of activities. I waited. Then the Catholic school contacted me about teaching a part-time computer class.

"I had only one computer class under my belt; how could I teach computers? The administrators didn't worry about my lack of experience because the computer company would provide training. They wanted someone who understood curriculum, knew about child development, and could work well with faculty and staff. My first assignment would be to teach computer classes to kindergarten through fifth grade on a part-time basis.

"I accepted. After one year, other doors were opened. The parochial school wanted to start a pre-kindergarten program. With my kindergarten experience and master's degree in early childhood education, they felt I was qualified to set up this program. Now in our second year of pre-kindergarten classes, I find it very satisfying to teach in this urban Catholic school. Although my students do speak English, I'm going to take Spanish classes!"

Back to Laura

In the '80s and '90s—

"Laura, let's pick up where you left off earlier. Once you hit 50, did you experience job discrimination? " Alli inquires, as she refers to her notes.

Laura responds, "That's hard to say. After years of counseling in an ideal school setting in Iowa, I chose not to seek a counseling position when we moved to a new city with its drug and gang problems. White, a Northerner, and 50, I felt I experienced some reverse discrimination in a city where whites are in the minority.

"So I decided to do something totally different. I thought it would be challenging to work in a hotel Catering Division. I was offered positions at both luxury hotels where I applied. My talented and moody French chef boss showed his amorous side by standing behind my computer chair to massage my aching neck and shoulders. It didn't help that my hot flashes raised such havoc that my suit jacket was on and off a hundred times a day—at my bidding, not my boss's! It didn't take me long to realize this was a dead-end job for me.

"Next, I became Administrative Assistant to the president of a world-class international resort consulting firm. It was a pleasure to work in a company with several other people about my age. What a wonderful education to learn about exotic places and a whole new world of finance and wealth, as well as chicanery.

"For the past few years, my husband and I have worked together. He travels a great deal consulting with church denominations, and we both work out of our home. He has his space, and I have mine! A home office eliminates worry about working late at night in an office building. We both write books. At age 57, I started my own publishing company. Not everyone would like to start a new vocation at our age, but it certainly is challenging. Alli, remember that you are never too old to do something new, if that is your desire."

Ann

Serving Four Terms on City Council

"Ann, tell us how you happened to run for city council," says Alli. "Your bid for a city council seat was well in advance of current trends toward women in politics."

Ann begins. "I was involved in a zoning issue in our neighborhood and became the spokesperson for the group. The zoning issue revolved around a property owned by a wealthy man who wanted to tear down the house and build an apartment building. He had tried several times in the past to have the zoning law changed. The neighbors, of course, were opposed to high density housing next door or across the street, and we prevailed in what was to be this final fight against the zoning change. After being defeated this time, the man sold the property and the problem was solved; it was a great victory.

"That experience made me realize that a lot of people feel inadequate in their ability to deal with the power and processes of even local government. One person against city hall can be intimidating.

"The zoning victory helped me decide that I wanted to work for people who needed help in dealing with city government. I conducted a door-to-door campaign, which was a fantastic experience. The first time I ran I was involved in a primary race against two men, one of whom was a strong union member. But I won with 60 percent of the vote in a blue-collar union environment and went on to serve three additional two-year terms.

"It's interesting that you mentioned that my bid for the council seat in 1980 preceded popular trends of women in politics. When I was campaigning, I was often greeted with the statement: 'I'll vote for you because you're a woman.' The perception was, and still is, that women are more honest and don't get involved in the 'good ol' boys' networks.

"During my tenure on the city council, I earned a reputation for always doing my homework—for knowing what I was voting on and why. It became a habit with me to keep notes from various meetings, so I always had a reference. Other people became aware that I had a written record, and I could challenge persons who attempted to be misleading about what had happened at a meeting."

"You were also employed during this time?" asks Alli.

"Simultaneously I worked at a technical college coordinating seminars and conferences. Originally, it was a part-time job, but it became full time. I was able to increase the success ratio of the seminars from 40 percent to 90 percent during the eight years I was there, which was very rewarding. The nature of the job demanded a flex schedule which was ideal for me because it allowed me to also attend all of the day-time and evening meetings as a member of the City Council."

"I've always wanted to spend time in Washington, D.C. Tell us about your current work there," Alli requests.

Ann: Now—

"Currently, I am working in government relations for a trade association. My work involves tracking legislation on federal and state issues, attending hearings on 'the Hill,' and coordinating grass-roots efforts in the states. I also take classes at George Washington University in their Washington Representatives Program, which is a lobbying skills program."

Alli asks, "Is there a degree offered in lobbying?"

Ann answers, "It's a certificate program, but I'm just taking classes I am interested in. The certificate is not important to me. Recently, I have also had the opportunity to become involved in acting in corporate and industrial videos and cable TV programs."

"How interesting. Your acting talents are put to use in another medium besides community theater," comments Alli.

Sexual Harassment—

Mainly a 1990s Problem?

Continuing, Alli says, "I hear a lot about sexual harassment in the work place these days. Did any of you suffer from such treatment over the years?"

Laura frowns. "Yes. This is such a sensitive matter, but it has certainly been brought to the public's attention recently with the Thomas/Hill hearings and numerous lawsuits. For me personally, the most blatant case of sexual harassment came from a school superintendent of a large and highly-rated school district. I'm sure that a man like this picks on a woman who has too much to lose if the situation is brought to the public's attention or if a lawsuit is filed. It is his word (a highly-respected school superintendent) against your word (an employee). This particular man was well aware that I was married, had several children, and was a devout Christian.

"His campaign began by easy conversation. Several times he came to my office at school to pressure me to go out with him. He'd close the door and make advances. My principal saw him make approaches, but he had no idea of the extent of his pursuit. For some reason, I think the principal saw it more as a threat to him. No matter how rude, how obnoxious I became, this man returned."

"Why didn't you report it?" asks Alli.

"Aside from the '70s environment, it's a little like rape. Despite the evidence, people continue to wonder what *you* did to bring this on. Secondly, as a mother and a working wife, I didn't have the time, money, or emotional energy to take on such a horrendous challenge. Our children would have been embarrassed had I 'gone public.' This influential man had political savvy, and I was a novice; he would have managed to make me the fool. Our family's reputation was too important for us."

Alli interrupts, "But ignoring it only contributes to nurturing sexual harassment in the work place."

"Frankly, my husband and I dealt with it privately. But, in those days, it would have been a no-win situation to make a public issue of it. You may think me a coward, but our family had more important uses for our energies," Laura adds wearily.

Domestic Engineers

Thanking Laura, Alli moves on to related topic. "All of you worked outside the home at some point in your married lives, and most of you took time off to stay at home while raising a family. Some of you continued your education and picked up on new careers when your children left home. Did those of you who stayed home feel that your education was being wasted? Or, that your life was boring?"

Audrey

Then—

Audrey replies, "I taught for five years after we were married, but after the arrival of our first son, I stayed at home. Becoming parents of three children within four years made the days full and the demands many. Since Art was in sales, he was gone several nights a week. We felt it was important for me to be available for our children's needs, activities, and routines during those busy growing-up years.

"We've moved ten times because of career changes and transfers. Certainly making ten different houses home—relocating, decorating, furnishing, and getting acquainted—has been challenging and satisfying. Had I been a working mom, it would have been difficult to extend the hospitality to friends and relatives that was so important to us.

"I was able to take an active part at church and maintain my commitment to continuous learning, not only through occasional courses but by focusing on my growth in what George Gallup, Jr. calls 'faith literacy.' I have become so dedicated to that growth that my husband teases me about having earned the 'L.T.' degree, for 'Lay Theologian.'

"In retrospect, I would say that my lifelong zest for growth in Biblical and doctrinal understanding has been a crucial ingredient in elevating my 'Homemaker' role to a high sense of vocation—my Christian 'calling.'"

Audrey: Now—

"Art is now retired, and we've moved back to our home town in Minnesota. This long-building sense of my vocation in our home assures both of us that our useful life hasn't been put out to pasture."

Celia

A Deliberate Decision Then and Now—

Alli turns to Celia. "You are another long-term 'domestic engineer.' Did you ever feel pressured into working outside the home?"

"No, my staying at home was a deliberate decision. I was married at Christmas time, and I ended my teaching career at the end of that school year. Staying home to raise our children through high school claimed the next twenty years. Since there was an overabundance of elementary teachers, I wasn't tempted to go back into teaching. Had there been a shortage of teachers, or had we felt financially strapped, I would have re-entered the work force. But, we chose to live on one salary. Living in a small town when our children were in school probably made it easier to do just that.

"Like Audrey, I think the freedom to volunteer for meaningful church and community projects is one of the rewards of not working full time outside the home. My church involvement has taken on enormous proportions, and I couldn't have been so involved had I been employed full time. Like Audrey, I've grown a lot in my faith literacy.

"My life has been happy and satisfying as a homemaker. I have no regrets."

Hobbies Anyone?

Alli notes, "All of you Blue Garter Club members remain very active in church and community activities. What about other pursuits?"

Ann responds: "I have loved working in community theatre wherever we have lived. I've acted in a number of plays, but I have been involved in all of the arts."

Marilyn takes a different tack. "For women of all ages, among the most important priorities is to keep healthy. Since both my parents died of heart attacks and two of my sisters have had bouts with breast cancer, I'm very aware of the family medical history I carry with me. Therefore, I spend my spare time in exercise and furthering my health discipline."

"So do I," adds Sarah. "We go to the YMCA three days a week to use the exercise equipment there."

Alli says, "Now I know why you all look so good! How about golf? Some of you are tournament players. Barbara?"

"John bought me golf clubs before we were married so I wouldn't have to be a 'golf widow.' I've won the ladies' golf tournament many times. Since golf is a big thing in our family, we take golfing vacations."

Looking at Aimee and Sally, Alli asks, "Are there are more golfers in the group?" Aimee simply says, "Yes." Sally adds, "Our whole family enjoys golf when they get together."

"Golfing and bowling have been a part of our leisure activities," says Celia, "but square dancing provides our best exercise. Square dancing through community education classes opened up a whole vista of friendships and fun for us. We have traveled throughout the state and into Canada for square-dancing events. We even went on a Caribbean cruise for square dancers. My sewing machine also got plenty of exercise when I sewed attire for these events."

"What diverse interests you have, amidst so many significant commonalities," All comments. "Collectively, you have lived in most states across America, as well as in Europe and the Far East. I'm impressed! Your combined longevity totals nearly eight hundred years. But, like Methuselah, God isn't finished with you, yet!"

Go For It!

Marilyn looks startled. "Eight hundred years!" A hearty laugh erupts around the Blue Garter Club. "But I think we'll all agree that we still have a lot of living—and growing—left to do. What a refreshing attitude in this group. Several of us were students and even got advanced degrees in our mid fifties. *Go for it!* If you want to start a new career, don't let age deter you. *Go for it!*"

Marilyn is insistent. "I had my teeth straightened at a late age—wearing braces and going through the whole teenage thing! People said, 'If you can go through two years of braces at your age, so can I!' Age need not be a deterrent to any form of self-improvement. *Go for it!*"

Sarah adds, "I was inspired by a gentlemen who learned to play the piano while in his seventies. Age didn't deter him."

Alli shakes her head in amazement as she summarizes. "One of the purposes of this chapter was to emphasize the need to grow, to continue pursuits, and to try new things as long as you desire. You seem to be in agreement that age is irrelevant. You have inspired me to take off my blinders and view your generation in an entirely different light. Before this weekend, I thought of people in their fifties as being kind of old. *Go for it,* ladies! I know *I* will when I'm your age, thanks to your inspiration!"

And now to a sobering chapter of life . . .

9

Till Death
Do Us Part

It's Over

It's over . . . Oh, it's over.
The relationship that once was so good is now gone.
I wonder why . . .
And yet sometimes, I am relieved.

There was tension
. . . there was uncertainty;
There was the never ending ache:
The ache of knowing it would soon end.
The ache of seeing the good fall apart.
The ache of feeling so helpless . . .

Oh where does one turn
When everything seems so very bleak?
When dark clouds cover even the happy times?
Good memories cast a soft light on the dark
clouds, and
Good friends try to brighten the colors of the
day.

But only God, through me, can erase the black
*   and the bleak;*
Only His Spirit can wrap me in pure white
*   clouds*
*   of security and peace.*

These clouds, untouched by human hands,
Remain the strong arm of God's love
*   streaming from the heavens.*
Once more . . . I am protected!

© Dee Hoff Larson

* * *

Alli has looked forward to this session for reasons that are at once more personal, yet distinct from most of the group. Two Blue Garter Club members have been widowed, and they are going to share their experiences. Alli is eager to learn how they have coped, as parents and spouses. It's been twenty years since Alli's mother's death; her father has never remarried. Recognizing that she and the others will sit quietly while Dana and Kate tell their stories, Alli begins.

"When you repeated your marriage vows and said 'Till death do us part,' you declared your faith and trust that God would give you many years together in marriage." Alli looks at 14 women, all blessed with long marriages. "Losing one's mate can be the most stressful event anyone goes through—either husband or wife. The two widows among you were married for 30 and 33 years. Yet their husbands died in the prime of life, leaving behind widows in mid-life. Dana, why don't you tell us what it has been like, and then Kate will follow." Alli gestures toward Dana, who is ready to begin.

Dana and Chris

"Chris was only 56 when he died," begins Dana, "There had been a number of early deaths from heart disease in his family. His dad was 25 when he died. An aunt and uncle died in their fifties from heart disease. Another aunt had heart problems but, with treatment, lived a normal life. It's unclear when his heart problems started, but at age 20, Chris passed his Air Force physical without incident. For many years he was a school principal and superintendent. After a stressful school building program, Chris decided to go into the insurance business."

A New Career; A New Lease on Life

"During a physical examination required for promotion to district manager in the insurance company, he was told that at some point he had had a heart attack. This news came as a shock, but alerted us to his potential heart problems. At that time, I was caring for my aging parents and monitoring their health and medications. We would sit around the table and make a game out of taking everyone's pulse. Taking Chris' pulse caused me concern. It was strange; not steady like it should be. One night he complained of indigestion, and the doctor ordered him to the hospital for ten days of complete bed rest to avert a heart attack. An angiogram revealed the need for his triple by-pass heart surgery. Ironically, our little game of taking everyone's pulse was what prompted Chris to see the doctor; it is doubtful he would have survived a massive coronary. Again, it makes me think of how God works in mysterious ways.

"After heart surgery in his mid-forties, Chris seemed to have a new lease on life. He was such an optimist and because he had been given a new start, he wanted to live life to the fullest. The by-pass surgery allowed him several more years that were really good for us.

"We all valued life more because of Chris' health. Although his heart problems should have slowed him down, Chris was able to accomplish a lot. Doctors commented that they didn't know how he managed to do as much as he did, based on his test results."

Mid-life: Another Career Opportunity

"Going into our own jewelry business was really a third career for Chris. We made the change to reduce his stress resulting from corporate sales expectations in insurance. Blessed with abilities in many areas, he learned a whole new trade at age 46. Adept with his hands, he was very good at working with small jewelry pieces. However, it soon became apparent to me that although he was his own boss, Chris was creating his own stress. Jewelry work wasn't physically strenuous, but he demanded a great deal of himself and did not want to admit he needed help.

"Five years after Chris had that heart surgery, we decided to move to Arizona. Stress was escalating for us because of economic conditions; we were forced to sell our jewelry business in Minnesota. We purchased a jewelry business in Arizona. Unfortunately, we were unable to sell our Minnesota home and other property. The dilemma produced too much negative stress for someone with heart problems."

That Special Chemical

"Chris was apparently suffering congestive heart failure when we arrived in Arizona. His ankles were huge from retaining fluids, but he managed to lose 45 pounds after his physician got him on the proper diuretic. The doctor said he didn't know what kept this man going, that he must have a special chemical in his body! That special chemical was his faith in God and his strong desire to give something back to the world after he had been given a second chance through by-pass surgery. Chris was always optimistic!

"We arrived in Arizona full of enthusiasm about having our own business, but we were apprehensive about leaving our relatives up north, particularly Chris' mother and sister. His sister's husband died of cancer right after we moved, and she felt so alone without Chris. Knowing we couldn't be there when someone far away needed us made us feel very guilty. The timing of our move was far from ideal, but sometimes we can't control these things.

"My only relative living in Arizona was a cousin I didn't know, but we became great friends. We clicked! It was wonderful to have family so far from Minnesota. We were together for holidays. On Christmas Eve the first year, we had twelve people at our home for dinner. Not expecting to even know twelve people in Arizona, I had sold my big table. We had to round up card tables so we could all sit down together."

And Then Came the Bankruptcy

"Times were tough for us in Arizona. Trying to promote a slumping business was tough; coping with Chris' health problems was tough; and being so far away from Chris' family was tough. Although the business we bought in Arizona had seemed promising, it was misrepresented to us. We lost it, along with our Minnesota property, in a bankruptcy proceeding. Bankruptcy is the most demeaning thing I have ever been through. I felt like an insect being stepped on but left alive to struggle."

Where Are You, God?

"At one of the apartments where we lived, we became friends with a wonderful Jewish couple. Saul and Norma were always able to see both sides of an issue and would always give two views: this view and, 'on the other hand.' On one occasion during our business problems, I was particularly frustrated and wondered why God was putting us through such turmoil. Pounding on my kitchen table I said to Norma, 'Where is my God when I need Him now?' She answered, 'He's right here where He has been all along.' God had not forsaken us. I was reminded of the Bible verse that says God does not allow a person to go through more than they can handle, but He provides the means to get through it."

Swinging Doors: Open, Closed, Open, Closed

"When our own store closed, Chris was hired by another store, so we felt that God had opened another door for us. We moved several times within the city, trying to live close enough to the store so Chris wouldn't have far to drive. About the time we got settled into this latest home near the store, *that* store also closed. Now what do we do?

"Well, God opened yet another opportunity for us. Chris was hired by the same company for one of their stores in Phoenix. The job market was very bleak for me at age 51, but once again I knew God had intervened on my behalf. Norma was a volunteer in the outpatient admitting department at a large hospital. Accompanying her to the hospital one day, I filled out employment application materials, and later sat with her, observing. Ironically, a position as emergency admitting clerk opened up while I was there. The personnel department interviewed me and hired me on the spot. Later I learned there had been 75 applicants for that position. Finding employment was a tremendous relief to me and further provided me with the assurance that God would help us through these difficult times. Some people might say I was lucky or that I was at the right place at the right time. True. But . . . who led me to the right place at the right time? God . . . and a Jew!"

Endurance: This Too Shall Pass

"I came to realize that God allows people to go through stages and varieties of hardship so they will know what it is like and to get into condition for whatever else may come their way. Or later to help someone else who is having the same tough time. The word 'endurance' seemed to pop out at me from various sources, and it came to mean for me: 'this too shall pass.'

"So far God had asked me to endure trials such as parents who were ill and totally dependent on me, their only child; a husband's poor health; a business failure; a son's divorce; and a daughter with relationship problems. Not knowing that the worst was yet to come, I just kept moving forward and praying."

The Beginning of the End

"In Phoenix, Chris saw a cardiologist on a regular basis. We were told there was a possibility that he could be a candidate for a heart transplant. He had also been diagnosed as having adult-onset diabetes. The doctor advised him not to travel outside the city, in case he needed to be near an emergency facility. Ignoring his doctor's advice, we took one short trip into the mountains. Driving on bumpy roads, I was fearful of having a flat tire which neither of us could change and worried that the intense heat would cause problems for Chris; I fussed the whole time. It was the last time he saw those beautiful mountains.

"Although Chris looked good, he became very weary. Many times we were ready to leave for church, but he couldn't make it. His blood pressure would drop extremely low; he would become dizzy and almost collapse. The beginning of the end was Palm Sunday of 1987 when he became ill during church. His blood sugar was very high— in the 800's, and we had to take him to the hospital. Thinking his blood sugar was low, I had given him a doughnut and orange juice. Although the doctor assured me it wasn't so bad, I felt like such a dope when I found out what was wrong.

"At this point, the cardiologist told Chris that he should retire. Accepting this idea took a while, but he finally went on disability six months before he died.

"Chris drove me to work the day he died. He didn't feel well that week; he thought he was getting the flu. Even a trip to the cardiologist's office earlier in the week didn't reveal anything different, and he scheduled another appointment later that day.

"All morning at work I was like a caged animal. My concentration was gone. My uneasy feeling couldn't be explained. When Chris didn't call during the morning, I tried calling him. No answer. Calling the cardiologist's office, another doctor's office, and the store where he previously worked brought the same response: he hadn't been there.

"Sensing my anxiety as we lunched together, Shirley, a co-worker, offered to take me home. Thinking Chris might have called while we were out, I suggested waiting until we got back to the office.

"In the meantime, Betty, another co-worker aware of my uneasiness, called her husband and asked him to go to our home to see if the car was there. The car was in the carport and the door to our house was unlocked, so he went in when there was no answer to the doorbell. Standing guard at the bedroom door, Abby, our golden retriever, wouldn't let him go any further. However, he could see Chris lying on the bed. Calling 911 from the kitchen phone brought the paramedics, the fire department, and a police car to the house. They managed to persuade Abby to leave her guard post and go out on the patio."

When Reality Struck

"My friends at work were driving me home by this time. The paramedics and fire truck left as soon as it was obvious nothing could be done, but the police waited for me. Seeing the police car in front of my home, it still didn't register that something was wrong. Being trained for this type of trauma, the policeman was very kind and caring as he talked to me outside, telling me my husband was dead. I remember screaming.

"Calming down, I started toward the house, but at first the policeman didn't want me to go in. Death was not a stranger to me, I told him—my parents had both died. He consented, and I went in to say good-bye. It appeared that Chris had been dead for awhile. He looked peaceful, as though the moment of death came painlessly. For that I am grateful."

Now to Tell our Children

"Marla had been notified at work and came home. She came running into the bedroom yelling, 'Mother, Mother.' Unfortunately, she hadn't been told that her dad's body was still lying on the bed. Her grief was overwhelming. Marla had been very close to her father.

"The first order of business was to inform Kevin, who was in Germany, of his father's death. He had recently remarried, and I had never met my new daughter-in-law. Just before the funeral, I met Kevin's new bride for the first time."

Decisions Which Cannot Wait

"The first of many decisions to be made was to determine where the funeral and burial would take place. Chris and I had previously talked about cremation in general terms, but we had never really talked about his death, or what I should do in the event of his death. He was so optimistic; I think he expected to have a heart transplant and another lease on life.

"Deciding against cremation, we agreed to have the funeral and burial in Minnesota. I felt it would help Kevin to better accept his father's death if he could view the body. Also, since Chris' mother didn't approve of cremation, I felt it necessary to consider her feelings. I haven't been sorry."

. . . And Then Came the Great Comforter

"Trying to clear my head the day after Chris died, I took Abby out for a walk. I prayed. Stopping in front of my neighbor's house, the strangest thing happened to me. I became totally wrapped in a cloud-like substance; a soft white matter was surrounding me and seemingly hugging me. Looking up toward heaven, it was like God telling me that His strong arms surrounded me, assuring me that everything would be all right. My mind was suddenly eased while, at the same time, filled with questions. What had happened? What was the cloud-like substance? Was it the Holy Spirit? What was the Holy Spirit trying to tell me? Heading back to my house and ready to make decisions, I felt the Great Comforter had indeed given me strength to face my immediate future and a promise of strength thereafter."

Alli interrupts briefly, asking, "What were some of the immediate changes you had to make after Chris' death? Did you continue to live in your home? Did you continue to work at the hospital? Did you need transportation to work?"

Now I Am A Widow—

"After the funeral I had to face realities about how I would live, how I would make ends meet. The life insurance company had informed me that there were no funds, that Chris' policy had lapsed because one premium had not been paid. How could this be? I couldn't afford our present home, so I moved in with my friend, Karen, for a four-month stay. Karen could look at things objectively. Managing financially was difficult, and I sold many things just to have money. Later I regretted doing that. Unaccustomed to driving in city traffic required new courage and resolve, but I found out it wasn't so hard.

"Living with Karen was helpful, but it also gave me a feeling of living in limbo. My first Christmas as a widow was spent with Karen. Although she made the holiday as joyful as possible under the circumstances, it was a difficult Christmas for me. Finally, I moved into my own townhouse, and then I had to face the reality of being alone. Now it was just me and Abby."

Reflections

"In many ways I was thankful Chris did not have to be hooked up to life-support systems. It was easier for him to go this way, but maybe a little harder on the family because we didn't expect it. Even when you know someone is very ill and won't live long, death is still a shock. I have never blamed God for Chris' death in the prime of life. I simply accepted it.

"Loneliness was my constant companion in the beginning, even in the company of friends. It comes and goes like waves in the ocean and is difficult to deal with. Daily I fight depression. I have to force myself to seek outside contacts and worthwhile activities. Helping other people is very important to me. The passage of time does help to ease the loneliness, but it never goes away completely. A widow often feels like a fifth-wheel, the extra, or the outsider. Although I experience the feeling of being incomplete without Chris, nevertheless, I'm still happiest in the company of married couples."

Grief Classes

Alli asks. "Did you attend grief classes, Dana?"

"Yes. Grief classes were helpful and informative. I don't know how a person copes with a loved one's death without a Christian faith. The class leader read a list of physical ailments that can be brought on by grief. It's kind of funny, but it isn't really—I had almost all of the ailments. I'm terribly impatient with not feeling well; after all, an aspirin *should* take care of any aches and pains. Although my condition has improved, I find that when adversity strikes, my depression returns and I have physical setbacks. I try to deal with problems as they come up, as I can't afford to dwell on them. Other widows have told me they feel they're losing their minds as they suffer from insomnia and constant restlessness. Grief doesn't just disappear; like loneliness, it passes and it returns.

"People grieve for different reasons. My situation might be the most typical, but I feel that my grief was minimal compared to what one woman had to deal with. This woman had been gang raped. She had so much more to struggle with than I did. Not only did she have to try to forgive the people who had abused her in such a horrible way, but the road back toward renewing her own sense of self worth was a long road to travel. Many times I have prayed for that woman."

"Dana, please don't refer to your own grief as minimal," counsels Laura. "It's just that your grief had fewer explosive ingredients than the rape victim's grief."

"That's true. Thanks for that," answers Dana.

God Took Care of Me

Alli picks up the pace, "This is a delicate question, Dana, but after all your financial difficulties, how did you manage to get back on your feet?"

"Good news came from the insurance company. A double premium payment had been paid at one point, making the policy current. So I was informed that payments would be made to the beneficiary after all. Again, I thought of how God had told me in that strange cloud-like embrace that everything would be all right."

"Can you share more about that cloud-like experience, Dana?" questions Claudia.

"The experience was exactly as I described it earlier—a sense of being wrapped in a cloud-like substance—but it continued to be a mystery to me. I felt strongly that a message was given to me during that strange happening. I wanted an explanation, and I struggled with various ideas. One book suggested that widows sometimes have hallucinations. No way was I *hallucinating*!

"I approached several pastors for an interpretation of what had happened. None of them had anything special to say. Finally, one pastor said, 'Don't discount the power of the Holy Spirit.' In my heart, I felt that it was the Holy Spirit and hearing a reinforcement of that possibility made me very happy. It was hard to believe that the Holy Spirit would come to such an ordinary person with such a personal message. Yet that's what I believe happened. The assurance that everything would be all right helped me get through the funeral without being in a daze of grief.

"That Holy Spirit experience is one of the most meaningful experiences I have ever had. Earlier, I read aloud 'It's Over,' the poem I wrote about Chris' death and the Holy Spirit giving me strength."

Alli breaks the silence. "Thank you for sharing your experience with us."

Loneliness

Loneliness is a feeling
   we must all at one time bear.
   A deep despair—
   does no one care
   about my loneliness?

How can one so richly blessed
   feel this terrible emptiness.
   Tired, discouraged, undernourished,
   starved of love that one time flourished.

The lines of communication are down.
   At times I feel I shall drown
   in empty words and empty phrases,
   in four walls and quiet places.

Is there no redemption, no escape?
   Into darkness I must gape—
   looking for a face with meaning:
   That can only be Christ's beaming.

No human being meets all my needs,
   I must look to one who bleeds.
   On Calvary's cross
   I'm not alone—
   My vacant prayers to Christ have flown.

My loneliness does not take flight,
   but strength to face my awful plight
   is given by the Christ who shares
   my hurts, my burdens and my cares.

— Lois Qualben

Kate and Dan

Looking at Kate, who is leaning forward, Alli says, "You seem to be ready to share your story with us, Kate."

"Yes, I am. In thinking about these two men who have died, there seem to be many similarities between them. Physically they were almost enough alike to be brothers; big men—over six feet tall, overweight, aggressive personalities in their drive to be super salesmen—and they were thinkers. Both were willing to take risks and willing to do different things businesswise. And both went through bankruptcy! They were also jovial and fun to be with, but probably didn't take enough time for relaxing activities."

The Silent Killer

"After a year-long battle with cancer, Dan died at age 54, the same age at which his father died from cancer. Several of Dan's uncles, aunts and cousins also died of cancer. Advances in cancer treatment in the 35 years since his dad died gave us hope that our generation would be spared.

"If the cancer had been diagnosed in the earliest stages, the outcome might have been different, but Dan had an excuse for every symptom. He began losing weight, but when I mentioned this, he said his diet was finally working. When he began looking jaundiced, he said it was a sun tan. His cough was an allergy!

"By the time he was willing to see a doctor, colon cancer had spread to his liver and lungs. Colon cancer is often called 'the silent killer.' Dan admitted that he honestly didn't realize he was so ill. Although surgery was performed, the doctors didn't think he would live more than a few months."

The Stress of Bankruptcy

"In retrospect, going through bankruptcy at age 36 was the most stressful event of our heretofore 'upward and onward' lives. Bankruptcy, like death, divorce, illness, accidents or losing a job is one of life's major stresses. Loss of livelihood can cause as intense suffering to a marriage or family as loss of life. Some research indicates that a major trauma can shut down the immune system enough to lead to heart disease, cancer and other terrible conditions. Our bankruptcy was a bitter experience. Having put all of our life savings, as well as Dan's retirement from a previous position, into our own grocery store, we were optimistic about success. Working every day—more than a hundred hours a week—did not change a bad economy, and we lost the store.

"I tried to bargain with God to allow us to keep our store and our house when I realized we were going under financially. My end of the bargain was to keep our house open to youth groups, to be active in church work, and anything else I could think of that might be pleasing to God. I realize now my bargaining was as misdirected as it was well intentioned.

"Knowing we had to move elsewhere produced another set of stressful circumstances. How would we cope with moving, starting over in a new job, uprooting our children from school? Besides, I was six months pregnant! Alone in the basement one day, I yelled at God, ticking off the problems we had so He would be sure to get the message! For a moment, I was ashamed of my lack of faith; then I realized if I didn't believe in my Lord that strongly, I couldn't have yelled at Him. Our lives had always been moving in forward gear. But at that moment, I realized circumstances had caused a shift to neutral and maybe into reverse. I cried, but soon learned to let go and let God take over my agendas.

"Dan didn't have the luxury of crying. He had a pregnant wife and five children to support, decisions to make. His mind was occupied with thoughts of how to arrange financing to keep the store going. Some friends said to him, 'If this was happening to me, I'd be so drunk!' Responding to talk like that, Dan said that he had never had a drink in his life, and he wasn't going to start now because that would make matters worse."

A Move: A New Career

"We moved to Fargo after our grocery store failed, and Dan went into the insurance business and continued in that business for more than 18 years, until his death in 1990. For 10 years I worked with him in the business; I managed the office and also became an agent.

"During the six years before his death, we ran the business from our home. The home office arrangement worked out especially well when Dan became ill. He could talk to clients on the phone and use his fax machine. When clients came to the house, he could give advice from his recliner, where he spent most of his waking hours. Conducting business this way continued until about four weeks before his death, when he could no longer work."

When Elderly Parents Outlive Their Children

"Dan's mother was already a widow when we were married. Living in Moorhead, she was happy when we moved to Fargo, and she spent a lot of time with us. About ten months before Dan's surgery, she fractured her pelvis, and we had her move in with us. We rearranged our house to make a bedroom for her in our dining room. She lived with us for fourteen months.

That provided me with a crash course in caring for a semi-invalid. When her strength returned, she was able to move into a nursing home six blocks away.

"While his mother was still living with us, Dan's cancer had progressed to a point where he would sleep a lot. His mother would watch him as he slept. Fearful that he had quit breathing, she would go over and touch him, waking him up. This finally became too stressful for both of them, and she decided to move. Living close by allowed her to spend time with Dan on a daily basis. They did very little talking. They just held hands.

"Having a child die is one of the hardest things a parent can go through, and it isn't any easier if the 'child' is 54 years old and the mother is 88. Parents do not expect to outlive their children. Before Dan died I said to him, 'You know I will take care of your mother, don't you?' He said, 'I know you will.'"

Hospice Allows Time for Good-byes

"In addition to Dan's mother, we had our own six children who also watched their father's slow death. Hospice allowed us to have Dan at home, which was a blessing to all of us. It allowed the children time to say their good-byes and to adjust to the idea of their father dying. Wanting everyone to be aware of the seriousness of his condition, I tried to answer all of their questions and keep them up to date as the disease progressed. Several times we sat in the living room talking about the possibility of his death, and what we were doing to try to save him.

"Because he was sick for a whole year, hundreds of friends and relatives stopped by to see him and reminisce. Dan was always surrounded by family, friends, and relatives who cared about him. What he enjoyed most was talking about fun times we had with these people. Being at home made this possible. Hospice is truly a wonderful concept.

"With a shunt in his heart, Dan was able to take some of his medication by injection into the tube. Hospice trained me to give medicine this way. A hospice nurse came over two or three times a week at first and every day toward the end. With her available to answer questions, I could be the primary caregiver.

"Dan didn't want to talk about how sick he really was. People would ask me how he was doing because if they asked him, his standard reply was 'Just fine' or 'Doing good' or 'Oh, finer than frog's hair!' Six weeks before his death, he was having extreme pain in his neck. The doctor prescribed morphine. Morphine is a great pain reliever, but it has terrible side effects. He couldn't get up, so he spent most of his time in his recliner."

A Service of Healing

"Going through the stages of grief before his death, we were still trying to save him. During this period of time, I found comfort in the Bible. Reading James 5:14-16 made me consider the possibility of having a healing service.

> "Is there anyone who is sick? He should send for the church elders, who will pray for him and rub olive oil on him in the name of the Lord. This prayer made in faith will heal the sick person; the Lord will restore him to health, and the sins he has committed will be forgiven. So, then confess your sins to one another and pray for one another, so that you will be healed. The prayer of a good person has a powerful effect." James 5:14-16 [RSV]

"After talking to the pastors of our church, we decided to have a healing prayer service for Dan and for others in need of healing. We used the 'Service of the Word for Healing' from the book, *Occasional Services*, published by Augsburg Publishing House. It is a service of communion and anointing with oil. About forty people, including all of our pastors, the elders of our church, friends, relatives and other people who were in need of healing prayers, came to our house for that beautiful service. By this time, we knew we had done absolutely everything we could to make Dan well and having a healing prayer service was a comfort to our family.

"In the next few days Dan said to me, 'Kate, I don't think I have any more pain. The side effects from the morphine are so bad that I don't think I want to take it any more.' When we learned that discontinuing the morphine would produce no withdrawal problems, Dan decided to quit taking it. He lived for four more weeks free of pain and with a clear mind. The prayer service had indeed been a healing service. In my prayer that day, I prayed 'God, please make Dan well.' But God answered my prayer in a different way. He answered my prayer by taking away Dan's pain. God is merciful!"

How Does a Person Face Their Own Death?

Alli asks a question. "Kate, can you share with us a little about Dan's state of mind as he lay dying?"

"'Gracefully' is the word I would use to describe how Dan accepted his own death; perhaps more gracefully than most people could accept their death being imminent. He asked the hospice nurse one day how long she thought he had, and she hesitated a moment before answering, 'From my experience, I think you have about three weeks.' His reply was, 'Oh, that's nice. I wondered how much longer I would have to go on like this.' Listening to this conversation made me wonder about the training the hospice nurses receive in answering questions like that. Then hearing Dan's reply also made me realize that he didn't want to live in this incapacitated condition and hoped it would end soon.

"The second and third nights before he died I prayed, 'God, make him well or take him home.' The last night I prayed, 'Take him home.' In 1990, Dan died one month and one day after our service of healing."

We Appreciated Having Visitors Come

Claudia speaks hesitatingly, "Kate, as you know, Martin and I were at the healing service. We both felt it was touching, inspirational, and beautiful. As I admitted to you before, it was difficult to visit your home and see Dan so ill, knowing this would be the last time we would see him. Not knowing how to approach an old friend who is dying, I put off going. It took prodding from other people and a phone call from you, Kate, to encourage me. Since then, I have been so grateful we were there."

Kate replies, "And we are grateful you were there, too. Even though it was difficult, visitors came. They knew it was appreciated by Dan and his family, and it brought them a certain peace to be able to say good-bye. Very few friends stayed away because they didn't know what to say. Dan was such a man's man—he had a group of men friends who stuck by us and helped us in whatever way they could to the very end. They served as pallbearers and have continued to be a support for our whole family."

Handling Grief Through Art

Alli keeps the topic on focus by asking, "Did you attend grief classes like Dana?"

"No. Perhaps we eased into our grief a little more slowly. Dana was unprepared for her husband's sudden death—it was thrust upon her. This probably makes grieving more intense when death comes. With Dan's health failing over a period of almost a year, we had time to grieve before his death. God had helped us do everything we could to save Dan's life, but it was time for him to die. We accept death as a part of life.

"We all grieve in different ways, but our son, Sterling, the artist, handled his grief through art. He painted several pictures depicting our family's grief. We also find comfort in a beautiful portrait drawn by a friend. My grief eased as I realized that I had to get on with my life and be ready to help other people who needed me— our children and Dan's mother. But we knew our life would be different without this wonderful husband, father, son."

Talking About the Deceased is Good Therapy

"It must be painful to talk about Dan," says Audrey.

"Widows do like to talk about their husbands, remembering the fun times and laughter. This is good therapy. People should never feel it is in poor taste to fondly mention the name of the deceased. A fond remembrance or a simple 'I'm so sorry' is appropriate and appreciated by a grieving family.

"Being the widow of a man who died of cancer does present a problem for me when I visit acquaintances now suffering from this or another possibly fatal disease. While the disease is in progress, it is so important that the family have hope for recovery. Unless the patient is a close friend, my visit could be taken as a reminder of my own husband's death. From my own experience, I remembered feeling very apprehensive about our future when a couple of widowed people, upon hearing of Dan's disease, said, 'I feel so badly for what you will have to go through.' At the time I had not yet accepted that Dan would die."

Long Illnesses Allow Time for Planning

"Because Dan knew for so long that he would die, he was involved in decisions regarding his funeral and burial. He selected favorite hymns for the funeral, decided where to be buried, made business decisions. One last thing I was able to do for him was to prepare a bulletin for the funeral service, including our family picture, various details and words of appreciation. We have memorialized Dan in many ways and places. I prepared an album with his last pictures, funeral pictures, documents, cards, and memorials. We lovingly remember him, our life together as a family, and the Christian example he provided."

For several seconds there is complete silence and somber expressions and Alli finally speaks. "Our heartfelt thanks . . . and God bless you and your family, Kate."

Life Without A Helpmate

"I'd like to ask several more questions of you two," Alli says. "What is your life like today, after surviving these past years without your husbands? Do you have any advice to offer to other women in your situation? What are your greatest fears and insecurities today?"

Dana speaks up first. "One eerie aspect of being without Chris is hearing his laugh whenever I hear a funny story or when something happens that I know would amuse him. Chris had a hearty laugh. It is still with me."

Kate responds to Alli's questions. "Life goes on much the same, except that Dan is not here. Dan knew about the needs of widows and children, so he saw to it that he had good insurance. I advise other women: 'Insist that your spouse has physicals.' I realize you can't force a spouse to visit his doctor if he's unwilling.

But you can make sure you have adequate insurance for family needs in the event the breadwinner dies. Know your financial situation; be aware of business dealings which involve you. Keep your head about you and do whatever needs to be done.

"I'm not sure I have any real fears and insecurities, so maybe I would substitute the word 'problems.' Becoming a widow at age 54, I was too young to retire. In our insurance business, Dan was the salesman, and I handled the paperwork. Since his death, I've had to learn the sales end of the business. It would've been easier had he been here to teach me.

"Keeping busy with family, business, church work, and housework prevents me from dwelling on my loneliness," concludes Kate.

"Kate said it very well. I agree with her," Dana says with a motion indicating she has nothing to add to Kate's remarks.

Alli appears to be fighting back tears as she speaks. "My dad was like a 'zombie' for weeks after my mother was killed. It was such a shock to him and to the rest of us. My grandmother took care of my brother and me; she tried to answer our questions and help us understand what happened. For a long time, I was angry with God; but gradually I began to turn to Him for strength and guidance in my life, and my anger left."

"Your mother's death affected all of us deeply, and we grieved for her," consoles Laura. "You were all in our prayers."

"Thank you. Your prayers helped us through that tragedy, even though I was too young to know it," Alli comments. "We hear expressions like 'towers of strength' or 'solid as a rock' and now I believe I have witnessed what those expressions really mean. Not only you two, but your dying husbands have shown such godly strength. You people have demonstrated how God sustained you through every episode of your lives, and I can certainly see it in the stories I have already heard."

Time is Short

Time is short
  when I can serve my children.
Lord, let me cherish each demand and
  enjoy the knowledge I am truly needed.
  For too soon will come the day when
  I must step aside and let them go their way—
Give me the grace to provide them
  with the proper tools.

Time is short
  when I can serve my husband.
Lord, help me to make his home a haven
  from unrest and desolation.
  A place where he finds the peace, the warmth,
  the love only a wife and family can give.
  An escape from the noise and confusion
  of our busy hectic world.

Time is short
  when I can serve my Master;
  A lifetime perhaps . . .
  but only He knows how long that will be.
Lord, give me the grace to live each day
  in such a truly blessed way
  that in later years,
  I need not feed on bitterness
  or regrets of all the opportunities gone by . .
  to love, to serve, to give—
Instead, I will remember that I knew
  time was short
  and I wasted none.

— Lois Qualben

10

Dedicated to the Christian Life

Time is Short

Time is short
  when I can serve my Master.
  A lifetime perhaps . . .
  but only He knows how long that will be.
Lord, give me the grace to live each day
  in such a truly blessed way
  that in later years I need not feed on bitterness
  or regrets of all the opportunities gone by . . .
  to love, to serve, to give.
Instead, I will remember that
  I knew time was short
  and I wasted none.

— Lois Qualben Verse 3

* * *

"Concordia College's stated purpose is to influence
the world by sending forth thoughtful and informed

men and women dedicated to the Christian life," begins Alli, "and the college's centennial motto 'Sent Forth' underscores that theme. You may not be among the big-time movers and shakers of our era, but you women are living proof that the college's purpose is being fulfilled. You care for the Christian atmosphere of your own homes and lead life styles that reflect intentional dedication to the Christian life. You have said that your Christian faith is the common bond that held this group together for 36 years. And you shared that faith through your Round Robin and other letters."

Alli focuses this chapter's direction. "You were raised in Christian homes; this helped establish you in the faith. Your college environment encouraged your concern to link faith with a life style you have maintained. Most of you came from strong Lutheran families, but not all of you have remained in that tradition. Nevertheless, a lifelong dedication to the Christian life describes all of you. This chapter won't dwell on your diverse church activities or your Sunday-world religion. Rather, let's emphasize your experience with faith at work in your Monday world. Tell me about your lifelong journey as it moves between both worlds. My contemporaries criticize Christians for just going to church on Sunday and then not applying the Gospel to the rest of their life outside of the church building."

Dana volunteers to start. "I have memories that go back to the age of three, when I was so proud of myself because I had managed to pray the whole Lord's Prayer in Sunday School for the first time. I couldn't wait to tell my mother. She always made sure that I had learned my Sunday School lesson by Saturday night, even though she was tired from working all day Saturday in our little family store. A child learns what really counts in a home by how (and for what) parents extend themselves when there's not much energy left. My mother's care for my Christian growth at such times has had a lasting impact on me.

"There have been times when people said to me something like, 'You must really love the Lord because it shows.' I guess they're referring to the fact that it feels like second nature to talk about my relationship with our Lord. Many people are embarrassed to speak about what Jesus means to them, but I enjoy expressing those feelings."

Bridging Sunday and Monday

Celia continues. "You noted that we've been sharing our faith through the letters we wrote. That often took the form of mentioning a church project we were working on, Bible study experiences, as well as discussing spiritual topics. For us, church is not only about Sunday, but has been a key to friendships and much of our social life. Some of us have moved a number of times. I doubt any of us waited for our new home church to come to us; instead, we sought it out and became active. If church weren't part of so many areas of our everyday lives, then I suppose religion would get chained to Sunday."

Kate agrees. "Moving to a new town, the first thing we did was find a church. At one new location the women's group met within a few days of our arrival, so I went to that meeting. The pastor's wife, who is still a good friend, couldn't believe I went by myself because most new people wait to be invited and for someone to pick them up. I told her I might be new to this church, but I am an old Christian. Whenever we moved to a new area, we felt right at home at the church we joined. Familiar worship styles and heritage help us feel at home, like part of an international family.

"Becoming active at a church not only encouraged and fed us spiritually, but also provided ready-made socializing," continues Kate. "We helped start a new church in South Dakota. We had a young couples club that was so much fun! This stands out in my mind as a strong example of how playful fellowship can combine with faith. The club was called 'The 79ers,' which meant that when the combined ages of the husband and wife reached 79, that couple had to quit!"

"So... did you also have a club for couples over forty? Like an 'Over The Hill Club'?" Alli asks.

"No. We probably would have started one, but we moved before we reached that age!" Kate laughs.

The Church is Only as Strong as its Body

"We also are charter members of a church," says Claudia. "We moved several times so we have belonged to different churches. I agree about taking the initiative to join a church instead of waiting for a church to seek you out. Although we stayed Lutheran all these years, we have enjoyed a variety of worship practices.

"Uprooted from strongly Lutheran Midwest culture to a western state with a very small Lutheran population was an eye opener. We joined a small Lutheran church in a community where we were definitely in the minority and the dominant religion, Mormonism, was radically different from ours. Lutheran pastors were few and far between, so we learned the importance of lay leadership. While we were there, our pastor accepted a call to another parish. Our congregation had to rely on its lay leadership strengths to provide services each Sunday. Interim pastors are often used in such situations, but none was available. In times like that, it really hits you that the church is neither a building nor its aggregate membership, but the Body of Christ— bigger than all of us put together."

"Did the pastoral vacancy bring your members closer together?" asks Laura. "I would think the congregation had to put aside petty differences and really pull together to keep going."

"Yes," Claudia answers, "that's what happened. Although we had few members, our church had enough drive and interest to keep things going. We took part in every aspect of the worship service. You won't believe this, but I even preached a sermon one Sunday during that time! I would never have done that in the Midwest."

"Believe it, ladies," Elizabeth smirks. "Living with Claudia for two years, I found out how good she is at preaching!"

Laura adds, "Lay participation is crucial in every congregation, and an effective pastor will surely nurture that participation. Since we've moved 13 times, we've belonged to a number of different congregations. Like all lay people, I had some worthwhile competencies, so as a new member, I asked one pastor if there was some area of congregational life in which I could serve as a volunteer. His answer was, 'We're in pretty good shape right now.'"

"Did you become active in that church?" asks Alli.

"Not really. We attended services, Bible study and special events, and transported our kids to youth groups. The 'up side' is that I became more aware of a need to be more evangelical and caring throughout my daily work in Monday's world," answers Laura. "When we moved to Washington, D.C., we headed for a Lutheran church the very first Sunday. Our 13-year-old daughter was invited to a youth camp-out. She immediately found her niche in a new city. She joined their well-attended 6:30 a.m. Bible study and participated in the group's musical performance of 'Godspell,' which they later performed at the National Luther League Convention in New Orleans. Theirs was a spiritually-alive and Bible-centered youth group, thanks to an insightful pastor and willing lay support."

Looking around the room for those with other experiences, Alli extends her hand toward Sally.

Where Two or Three Have Been Gathered in My Name . . .

Sally responds. "My church has also been very important to me, and I've been active in almost every facet of it. One of the best things that ever happened to me was a small prayer fellowship we called '2-3 Prayer Group.' We met every week and always studied something in preparation for those times. Not only was it a boon for my personal spiritual growth, but it provided significant closeness and support when members needed it. We could be open with each other. Our sights were kept high, eliminating the self-centeredness that destroys so many ordinary support groups. Our 2-3 group changed over the years as people moved away or went back to work full time, but I could count on that high-level support when I needed it. We had our critics, people who fancied these were nothing more than gossip groups. I can honestly say ours was a prayer and spiritual-growth group."

Laura adds, "For years, my husband and I also belonged to a prayer group. Now a thousand miles from us, its other members keep us in their prayers, and we continue to pray for them."

"Church music solos and choir were my primary activity for many years," Dana recalls. "Now that I live in a major city and belong to a large church, I've gotten involved in church musicals. It's a fun departure from the pretty formal approach to church music we got at Concordia. But, it really lifts my spirit as we praise our Lord through His gift of music."

"When we begin comparing notes on church experiences, we've all done many of the same things," says Barbara. "And, we are old enough to remember when women couldn't serve in leadership capacities except for women's groups. Times have changed: I'm serving as deacon. In addition, I'm teaching a five-year adult Bible study. Becoming involved in the church very definitely becomes a way of life."

Renae speaks up. "Aside from teaching or serving on committees, I helped to do the needlepoint on a kneeler used at weddings. That project represented many hours of work. I enjoyed serving on my church's Fine Arts Committee. Our church has beautiful works of art— mosaics, stained glass, needlework, paintings, sculptures— and the committee set up an art gallery, changing work by local artists every six weeks. We conduct art tours periodically, especially when our church is host to various church meetings."

Church in the Military

"Renae, how did being in the military affect your membership in a church?" asks Alli.

"We moved a lot, but whenever we were in a small community we always joined a church right away. Military chapels don't seem to offer as much or get people as deeply involved as other churches. We didn't feel the closeness of church membership while overseas. However, two of our children were baptized by base chaplains."

The Individualized Worship Experience

Alli acknowledges Sarah. "After belonging to large Lutheran churches for years, a move and job change prompted us to join a small Lutheran mission congregation. Social activism was all the rage there. We got well acquainted with other members who also felt spiritually neglected. In the early 1970s, several of us began talking about the Charismatic movement and how much more alive in Christ its members were. We attended a Lutheran Conference on the Holy Spirit at the Minneapolis auditorium. Seeing a Catholic priest, Lutheran pastors, and other denominations' pastors sharing the same stage, joining together in praise and worship and even dancing up there, filled me with an excitement above and beyond doctrinal differences. It was both an exciting and a difficult time—difficult because there was resistance to the in-dwelling of the Holy Spirit, but exciting because doors were opened to hear and learn more. I experienced the baptism of the Holy Spirit, with the additional gift of speaking in tongues. Because I understood so little of its proper use, this prayer language took a while to develop. But it has been a great blessing for me. Many scriptures come alive for me as never before. Over the years, I have attended many more charismatic gatherings. Exciting is the only word I can find to describe this sense of being filled with the Holy Spirit."

Alli asks, "Sarah, do you still belong to a Lutheran church?"

"We now belong to a Pentecostal non-denominational church, which we joined as a result of our interest in the Charismatic movement. While the music is a far cry from Lutheran chorales, the message always centers on total commitment to the Lord and is clearly Bible-based. Our spirit-filled meetings also appeal to young people. Many people troubled with alcohol or drug problems and other traumatic events have gotten their lives and relationships together."

"Thanks, Sarah. You are proof that not all Blue Garter gals stayed stuck in Lutheran cement. Have others of you left Lutheranism while continuing your Christian life and growth? Aimee ?"

I Joined a Congregational Church

"Yes, I'm one of those. Greg was raised Presbyterian. There is no Presbyterian church where we live, so he was attending a Congregational church when we were married. For awhile, we went back and forth between 'his' church and 'my' church. Eventually we joined the Congregational church, not least because it was so much smaller and we felt 'needed' there. Over the years I have produced newsletters and the Sunday bulletins and have done other communication work for our church. This kind of service is what I do best. In the Upper Midwest, where Lutheran churches often get so large, a member can easily feel like little more than a number. My Christian faith hasn't been so institutionally rigid that I couldn't move into a non-Lutheran church, and I've been happy with that decision."

Are Lutherans Perceived as Lacking Warmth?

"I can identify with what Aimee is saying," begins Elizabeth, "about feeling like a number in a church with a large membership. My background is Moravian, but since attending a Lutheran college, I have been going to Lutheran churches for many years. Don was Presbyterian. My service to the church is similar to my service to society—teaching and making use of my art skills.

"We belonged to one Lutheran church where the pastor epitomized what we feel a pastor should be, but we felt like fish out of water in that church when he left after serving there 17 years. Fortunately for us, he returned several years later to serve another congregation a short distance away. Now we attend that church. We're not being 'Groupies' about him. It's just that our pastor has his priorities for ministry straight, and that has affected the way our congregation percolates. In spite of my involvement, I don't find Lutheran congregations to be very 'warm.' I don't know any more people in either of those two churches than I did three years ago."

"Lutheran churches have a reputation for being cold, so Elizabeth's comment doesn't surprise me," Sally adds.

Claudia injects, "Our own route around that stand-offish Lutheran coolness has been to seek out a small group affiliated with each new church we've joined. Bible study groups are especially good for getting acquainted."

Alli refers again to the topic of leaving the Lutheran church. She asks Ann about her religious preferences.

Outreach in this Congregational Church

"I joined the Congregational church because of its strong leadership role in the community. Their community outreach programs agreed with my thinking on the responsibilities of the church in our society. As a member of a Lutheran church, I served as a volunteer secretary in the church office. One of my tasks was to record the attendance of the parishioners at communion. It bothered me that the church considered it important to keep records of how often people publicly asked for forgiveness. As a mother of three young children and a Sunday School teacher, I also became concerned about what the church was teaching children about guilt, and I decided that I didn't want my children growing up in that kind of religious environment."

Alli interrupts. "I'm curious to know how hard it was for some of you to leave your Lutheran upbringing."

"Changing membership to our present congregation wasn't all that hard for us, given how strongly we felt about our children's religious health," Ann says.

Lay Ministry in Monday's World

"Laura mentioned Monday's ministries earlier," Audrey begins speaking. "We've been talking mostly about Sunday aspects of our churches' life. My feeling is that how we live throughout the week has to be as important as what we do on Sunday. I'm offended by Sunday church-goers who contradict what Christians believe by neglecting to live their faith in their work place and home."

Claudia injects, "I don't see any one denomination's members doing better than the others at overcoming this contradiction. But we've *got* to—beginning with fellow Christians standing by a family or individual in need. For example, when our friend lost his job, several men from our church took turns being 'God's Man' for him. Yes, he lost his job but, because of these men, he didn't lose his Christian sense of *vocation*."

In response to Alli's puzzled look, Laura says, "A person's Christian sense of vocation means that God brings us together with our work and lifts our occupation or vocation to a religious status for Christians. Our work glorifies Christ, and self-fulfillment is secondary."

Marilyn adds, "Most church members don't know how to reach out to those who hurt. Some parishioners may give sympathy and support, but I can't think of many who could fill those 'God's Man' shoes. Most folks just feel uncomfortable talking to someone who's suffering a job loss, so they chose to avoid the subject—or the person. This leaves the unemployed person alone to cope with loneliness and despair over loss of livelihood, a loss of self worth and purpose."

Alli says, "As I mentioned, my company is planning some layoffs. As a personnel counselor, I view the subject of vocational distress as critical. When I return home, I'm going to talk to my pastor about conducting Bible studies that will teach parishioners how to connect Sunday to Monday's world and how to help others in the midst of their job loss."

Should Our Church Play Society's Tunes?

Alli continues, "All of you grew up in small towns where the church was a prominent feature of community and personal lives. Several of you still live in similar surroundings. For those of you who live in large cities, how has your church life changed because of your location?"

With an edge in her voice, Laura comments, "I feel that churches aren't as sensitive as they should be to today's over-saturated working women, the splintered family, and exhausted husbands."

"What do you mean?" asks Alli.

Laura continues, "For the past 35 years, we've lived in large cities. The commuting costs in terms of time, money, and patience are enormous. Adults who commute an hour or more between work and home often have to work past the dinner hour and don't see their children until the following night. Some churches seem locked into an earlier era when commuting and business travel weren't facts of life for members. Now, more than half the members are in dual-vocation households with the husband *and* wife both working full time outside the home. Unfortunately, many churches persist on an activities-involvement track."

"Give us a 'for instance,'" Alli asks.

"It's easy to be critical of members who don't seem to be 'doing their part.' There must be sensitivity about people's time and energy limits; perhaps at a later time this working wife and mother will be better able to participate in activity-oriented events."

Ann adds, "Another facet of attending church in a large city is the kind of neighborhood in which your church is located. In Washington, D.C., I find it difficult to attend the church of my choice because the location—downtown—is not a safe area. Other denominations' churches are closer to my apartment, but I choose not to attend."

"We spent some time in Washington, D.C.," starts Claudia, "so I'm aware of what Ann is talking about.

Population shifts around the city often left churches in an area that took on a totally different character from what charter members had known. The Lutheran church we attended had a special concern for feeding the homeless. Back home nobody was used to homeless people seeking refuge, literally, at the church's doorstep. One entrance to the D.C. church we attended was no longer used, so the homeless could sit on the sheltered steps. Worshippers entering on Sunday mornings often were approached by homeless people asking for money. We'd give some, even though we wondered if it would go for a bottle of cheap wine. I'll tell you, those months really opened our eyes to a *lot* our church back home never knew about."

"Homeless people actually lying at your doorstep might be more common in the big cities, but small town churches also get called on for food and lodging for many needy people. We don't hear much about that ministry," adds Alli.

Alli looks at the two pastor's wives. "Laura and Marilyn, my mother's best friend was our pastor's wife until they moved, just before Mom's accident. What's it like to be a wife and mother living in Somebody Else's house?"

Roles of a Pastor's Wife

"When our first baby was two months old, 'Hilda' called to bitterly complain that I wasn't taking leadership of the women's groups," Laura begins. "She said I should get out more and not be with our baby so much. After waiting five years to have a baby, I was in heaven caring for my little one, and it was *never* my intention to lead the ladies!

"Out of guilt, I accepted Hilda's invitation to 'do' devotions at the next Women of the Church meeting.

Before that 10 a.m. occasion, I loaded playpen and baby into the car, drove to the other end of the city to pick up the speaker, and raced back. We arrived a bit later than we should have. Our baby was screaming, I was panting from lugging the playpen and baby down the basement stairs. The women pitied me when I gave devotions, as they mistook my quivering voice as fear rather than sheer exhaustion. None of them pressured me to give devotions after that.

"Whenever I was asked to do some presentation, I volunteered to write a play or a program or provide a singing group. I organized a group of seven pastors' wives (sextet and pianist), and wrote a musical stages-of-life program for Mother-Daughter banquets. We performed at churches in Chicago for the next six years. We had a great time doing it—and an even better time practicing! Our husbands joined us for monthly dinners, and ours became a closely-knit group of couples."

Alli asks Marilyn about her pastor's wife experience. "Jerome responded to his sense of Call into the ministry during his senior year at Concordia. I was teaching, and we were already planning to be married the summer after his graduation. His decision to enter the ministry was also a decision I had to prayerfully work out in my own mind—did I want to be a pastor's wife? Neither of us grew up in a parsonage, but as a teenager I took care of the pastor's baby.

"Quite aware of criticisms heaped on some children of small town pastors, I wasn't at all sure I wanted to raise a family in that kind of fish bowl. Often the congregation and also the community have had higher expectations of the pastor's children than of other children. A 'PK' (preacher's kid) has it tough. Parsonage parents themselves sometimes expect more of their own children. As Jerome and I decided to share our lives in the ministry, we also made a decision that we wouldn't expect more of our children than of any other children in the congregation.

"During our year of internship the red hymnal was being introduced. The organist of one of the congregations refused to use the red book. Jerome looked to me for help. Although I had never taken organ lessons, I do play the piano and thought I could eventually learn the organ pedals. I became the organist that year and helped the congregation get accustomed to the new liturgy. I have assisted in this way—sometimes on a moment's notice, but I didn't want to be a regular organist."

"Did you consider yourself—and your marriage— included in his Call, that it meant you were to become an unpaid assistant pastor?" asks Alli.

"No, definitely not. God called Jerome into the ministry and the church ordained him, not me," answers Marilyn. "Laura spoke for me, too, when she said she had no intention of leading the ladies. I believe, strongly, that the pastor's wife should be an active lay person among others who serve our Lord. No congregation should expect her to take on special responsibilities just because she is the pastor's wife. On the other hand, some church women don't want their pastor's wife to be a leader, because they jealously guard these leadership roles for themselves.

"I serve best in music, particularly children's music. A pastor's spouse might have expertise that would be beneficial to a congregation, but these talents sometimes can't be utilized because of a constitutional rule or strong feeling within that congregation. As a result, the pastor's spouse may be prevented from serving that church as well as she could. Being the pastor's spouse can be almost a form of punishment!"

"Please be more specific about that," Alli asks, noticing questioning expressions on several faces.

"For example, some church constitutions don't allow two people from the same family to serve on the same committee. Since the pastor is an ex-officio member of all committees in a small church, the pastor's spouse is excluded. This wouldn't be a problem in a larger church with several pastors, each responsible for a different committee. In one congregation Jerome served, I was nominated for a committee and I accepted. For awhile it was okay, until someone complained about two members of the same family being on the same committee; I had to resign.

"I'm Jerome's favorite sounding board for frustrations about the congregation. In one parish, Jerome was extremely busy. In fact, he was gone so much that Tom, as an adult, looks back on those days as the time when he never saw his dad. Even so, some members came to him to complain they didn't think he was working hard enough. Why? They had heard that he sat with his feet up on the desk. Assuming this meant he wasn't doing anything, they informed Jerome they were going to watch for awhile to see if he was, in fact, doing his job."

"Oh, good grief!" Audrey blurts out.

"Jerome has a habit of propping his feet up on the desk when he's reading, sermonizing or preparing for a meeting," Marilyn explains.

Moving Out of the Lutheran Stronghold

Alli looks at her notes. "We've alluded to your predominately Lutheran communities in the Upper Midwest. But many of you moved to other geographical areas where Lutheranism isn't nearly as strong. How was your spiritual life affected by such moves?"

Dana's hand goes up. "For me it has been like a breath of fresh air to become friends with people from other religious backgrounds. Having Jewish friends has been particularly gratifying to me."

"Our life has been so rich," says Marilyn, "and some of that enrichment came when we left Lutheranism's

Promised Land (Minnesota) and ventured into other regions."

"We've grown a lot, too, since leaving the Upper Midwest," says Claudia. "We became accustomed to more cooperation between various Christian churches on such things as summer Bible School programs and youth activities. And, we learned that not all Lutherans are Scandinavian with 'Uff-da' in their vocabularies!"

When Leaving Home Includes Leaving the Church

"Let's shift to another theme that concerns some of you," Alli suggests, looking at a group of mothers who have spoken openly about their parenting worries. "I refer to young adults from Christian homes who leave their church when they leave your home. Some parents use Bible passages in self-indictment—such as Proverbs 22:6. *'Train up a child in the way he should go and when he is old he will not depart from it.'* When your children quit going to church, you feel responsible."

Kate speaks up. "Maybe we should define 'old' in that verse. After all, our children are still in their twenties and thirties. My feeling is that we should be patient. When I look back to the early days of our marriage, we didn't go to church every Sunday. With both of us working, some Sundays seemed to be made for sleeping in, relaxing, and going on an outing. When we started a family, our priorities changed. Babies don't know Sundays are for sleeping in! A highlight of the week for a three year old is Sunday School. So we parents wouldn't think of depriving our little ones of this pleasure."

"Feeling guilty or blaming yourself because your adult child quit going to church is neither healthy nor appropriate." Sally leans forward and begins speaking. "I won't lay a guilt trip on myself or accept blame for my

adult children's choices. Years ago I made it clear to
them that I had raised them as best I could. Now they are
adults; their future is up to them. We have both active
and inactive church-goers among our children and,
ironically, two of our three church college grads don't
go!" Sally laughs nervously, but notices understanding
smiles on other faces. "Attending a church college can't
guarantee lifetime commitment to church participation."

Sarah breaks the silence, "God's timetable is different
than ours. I think 'patience' is the key word. Keep on
praying and believing that your child will again return
to the fold. God is faithful, and in His own good time,
our Lord will get through to them."

"I agree," Celia adds. "When a parent has planted the
seeds of Christian faithfulness and living in the Body of
Christ throughout her child's young life, those seeds
will bear fruit in time. We *do* have to be patient. For some
children the seeds need a longer time to grow, but
eventually they will flower. Let the Holy Spirit continue
his work in these people."

"While growing up, I knew a man who lived right
across the street from the church, but he never attended
worship services with his wife and family," Claudia
begins. "He claimed he attended church every Sunday
as a child and 'had enough church for a lifetime,' so he
quit going. For some reason, that story stuck in my
young mind. Years later I visited my home church, and
I was surprised to see this same man ushering. As I
yearn and pray for my own children to return to church,
I am blessed with the gift of hope as I remember this
fellow who returned after many years. Nevertheless, I
can't figure out why some children from church-going
families claim they had religion crammed down their
throats and want to get away from it, while other children grow up with a strong faith and continue growing
in the church."

Allie says, "Why young adults so often leave the church is a question many churches struggle with. Is it part of youthful rebellion or of their attempts at identity formation? Have churches failed to convince young people of Christianity's relevance to today's society? In my opinion, sometimes the church treats its young people as mutants outside of the congregation's mainstream and ministry. Without safety nets and reinforcement for their spiritual formation at church, the kids get busy elsewhere." Alli jabs at herself, "And I was one of those kids for a while."

Sarah mentions, "The non-traditional music in our spirit-filled services at our Pentecostal church appeals to young people. But we also expect more of them, spiritually, than nearby Lutheran churches do."

"Contemporary services appeal to many young people and provide a more positive experience for them," adds Celia.

"Stodgy Lutheran liturgy and 17th-century hymns can add up to a bad case of culture shock for this generation. Many of the hymns we sing in the Lutheran church are the tunes of folk music," says Audrey. "Martin Luther even used bar songs in some of his hymns, because these melodies were familiar to his audience. I think we have to be more open-minded about what can be done to encourage young people to 'own' church life. Providing a contemporary service option on a regular basis would be a start, but we also need to overhaul our entire view of teenagers' place in the Body of Christ."

"As long as the Christian message isn't corrupted, we should be willing to accept a different type of worship service once in a while. We might even start tapping our feet," Kate chimes in.

"Formats and style must not get in the way of worship, whether traditional or contemporary," starts Dana. "But if people aren't motivated from within themselves to attend church, they won't go. Praying for the Holy Spirit to work on the unchurched is still an important prayer."

"Trouble and worry also can be motivators, but I don't think that's what you have in mind, Dana." Barbara continues, "Openness to the Holy Spirit for strength in our everyday lives is what each of us wants—not only for ourselves but for our children. Contemporary services, programs, and structures: these can remove some obstacles. But they become hollow gimmicks without underlying reliance upon the Holy Spirit's work."

Laura volunteers. "Don't despair. So often those who have been brought up in Christian homes do eventually come back to the church in their own good time. A friend of mine abandoned church all through her twenties. She even joined a cult. But after she and her husband had their first child, the baby was baptized, and they have been dedicated Lutheran Christians ever since. A neighboring pastor's daughter also rejected church. But when her second child was born, and other children in the neighborhood were heading off to Sunday School, their family resumed active participation."

"Prayer and patience are important, I know," adds Claudia, "but while the years go by, my children are missing out. Yes, they believe in Jesus Christ. But their faith is still in the 'baby stage' and is not growing. Without spiritual nurture and guidance on a regular basis, without Bible reading and prayer, the world's temptations are speaking much louder to our children than is the faith in which they were raised. Will their faith be strong enough to endure when that childhood Christianity comes under pressure? And, indeed, Christianity is threatened! Look at the evil forces at work in our world today—Satan is thriving! I hope my children don't become the 'lukewarm' Christians the Bible refers to, but that is my fear because their faith is not being nourished. Besides, I find such joy in my spiritual life, such strength, hope, peace, and love, which I want my children to experience. As it is, they seem adrift, without a rudder. And the seas are getting rougher," Claudia concludes, eyes on her hands.

"Now, to recap: Godly patience. Keep praying. Don't blame yourself. Rely on the Holy Spirit's work in your children to bring them back into the fold." Alli is summarizing the responses. "And encouraging more insightful approaches to youth ministry. The religious ties that bind the next generation are unraveling in places, but none of you have given up on those ties becoming as strong as they were for you in college."

When Children Marry Outside our Religion.

"What are your feelings about one of your children marrying a non-Lutheran? Is that a problem for you?" Alli shifts the conversation.

"The important thing is to for them to find a Christian church that's best for them, for their spiritual growth," begins Dana. "It doesn't have to be Lutheran."

"I agree," Claudia adds. "My children know I would not object if they joined another denomination so long as it is Christian. Different worship styles suit the needs of different people. Even though I prefer traditional Lutheran worship and doctrine, my children might prefer something else. I can handle that!"

"My daughter 'turned' Catholic when she was married and this upset me for awhile," says Elizabeth. "However, their beautiful wedding service, which Carla and Bill wrote themselves, was taken from both our Lutheran hymnal and the Catholic hymnal. Presiding was Bill's art teacher who was a monk at a Catholic Boys' School. I asked for a copy of his wedding address because it was the most meaningful homily I have heard on Abiding."

"Tell us a little about it," Alli asks.

"Well, Webster defines 'abide' as *to stand fast, remain, to stay, reside, to await, to live up to an agreement,* or in other words it means *to be there.* He stressed that marriage meant being there for each other. Extending this concept, he emphasized the importance of family being there for them. And, further, how God is there for all of us. Somehow he even brought in Winnie the Pooh!"

Alli looks at Kate. "We've been talking about Lutheran children marrying Catholics, Methodists or Baptists. But, your daughter married a Muslim. Wasn't that difficult for you to deal with?"

"No. And I don't understand it, but it never did bother us. Although our son-in-law is Muslim, he said from the start that he wanted their children to be raised Christian since we live in a Christian country. He is from a well-to-do family in Iran, the son of a doctor who taught at Oxford. The family has many Christian friends and is very open to what we believe. We felt that if God brought this wonderful young man from the Middle East and this beautiful young woman from North Dakota to a meeting place in New York City, He must have a plan for their lives and we wouldn't interfere. They are happy together: a lively mix of Muslim and Christian, Persian and Norwegian."

Continuing with a laugh, Kate says, "We've come a long way from my growing-up years when relatives would regard a Protestant and Catholic couple as an unsound marriage. In fact, we have Catholic friends who didn't attend their son's wedding because he married a Methodist girl. Although they liked the girl, they felt that attending the wedding would put their stamp of approval on marriage to a non-Catholic and set a precedent for their other children to also marry 'outsiders.' I know they later regretted that decision."

Alli brings this discussion to a close. "In your discussion about this chapter, you have carried me to a close sense of that warm-hearted Lutheranism I knew from my mother, your classmate. It did mean so much to Dad and us kids during our ordeal after Mom's accident. Thank you for opening to me other lively facets of our belief, not least your godly discontent.

"One of my favorite verses in the Bible is Galatians 5:22. *"But the fruit of the Spirit is love, joy, peace, patience, kindness, goodness, faithfulness, gentleness, self-control; against such there is no law."* [RSV] I memorized that verse in confirmation class several years ago. Now I frequently ask the Holy Spirit to bring this fruit into abundance in my life. After hearing your testimony of faith, I believe the Holy Spirit is working in each of you, too."

11

How Did Your Life Unfold?

I Was There To Hear Your Borning Cry

I was there to hear your borning cry,
    I'll be there when you are old,
I rejoiced the day you were baptized,
    To see your life unfold.

I was there when you were but a child
    With a faith to suit you well;
In a blaze of light you wandered off
    To find where demons dwell.

When you heard the wonder of the word
    I was there to cheer you on,
You were raised to praise the living Lord,
    To whom you now belong.

If you find someone to share your time
    And you join your hearts as one,
I'll be there to make your verses rhyme
    From dusk till rising sun.

In the middle ages of your life,
  Not too old, no longer young,
I'll be there to guide you through the night,
  Complete what I've begun.

When the evening gently closes in
  And you shut your weary eyes,
I'll be there as I have always been
  With just one more surprise.

I was there to hear your borning cry,
  I'll be there when you are old.
I rejoiced the day you were baptized,
  To see your life unfold.

Used by permission. © 1985 John Ylvisaker,
Box 321, Waverly, Iowa 50677

* * *

"John Ylvisaker's beautiful hymn, *I Was There To Hear Your Borning Cry*, depicts God's presence through every stage of our lives. The Blue Garter Club members can certainly attest to that," states Alli as she starts the recorder for our conversation relating to the final chapter of this book. Referring to her notes, she sets the tone of this session. "Using the text of this hymn as points of reference, tell us about specific events or people that made a special impact on your life. You have already noted that you were raised in Christian homes, so you could also expand on that, if you wish.

"I hope you will keep one or more of these themes in mind: (1) How did your distinctive life unfold? (2) What events shaped your character? (3) What role did the choice of your church-relating college have in orienting your future?"

"I rejoiced the day you were baptized . . ."

"We have all joined with millions of other Christians in bringing our children to the baptismal font in their early months of life, just as our parents did for each of us. We all felt it was one of the most significant acts of love we could give to our babies," volunteers Laura. "Certainly one of the highlights of Jack's ministry has been to baptize our three children and our grandchild. How he *glows* about that."

Marilyn underscores their similar family experience, saying, "It was always an emotional experience for Jerome to baptize our children and our grandchildren. As for my own baptism, my sponsors were very special to me. Although we didn't observe the anniversary of my baptism, which is a fairly recent idea emphasized in many churches, I knew my sponsors well as they were active church members who I saw regularly. They were so attentive to me throughout my growing-up years; they made me feel very special. I felt close to them. My baptism was the focal point of this close relationship, which made me feel that baptism was, indeed, a foundational event in my life."

"I was there when you were but a child . . . "

"Sitting in her new rocking chair, our daughter was singing *Jesus Loves Me, This I Know...* to her newborn baby. This is a *deja vu* experience I shall never forget. I'm sure my mother sang that little song to me, as I did to our babies," Laura reminisces.

Celia moves on to another track. "Reflecting on the events that shaped me, my father's death when I was 13 is certainly paramount. As the eldest of five children—the youngest was only four years old—I felt a strong sense of responsibility, knowing that if anything happened to my mother, I would have to take over. This is a sobering and maturing experience for someone just 13 years old. Fortunately, my dad had paid off the farm where we lived, but my mother couldn't continue to operate it without him, so she rented it out. We moved into town, where she worked in a drug store. God provided strength not only to my mother, who now faced raising a family alone, but to these five children as well."

Alli looks very serious now. "You all noted the importance of your Christian homes, regular church and Sunday school as among the significant events in the molding of your life. *Come into my heart, Lord Jesus* was a life-changing song for your growing-up years. God was there for you."

"I was there to cheer you on . . . "

"How has God cheered you women on?" asks Alli with a smile.

"He works through people close to us to create opportunities, to open doors, to encourage, train, lead, and to pray," Kate responds. "During my teen years, Bible Camp had great impact. Bible Camp sessions came during haying season, a time when I was needed on the farm. My parents sacrificed a lot to let me attend camp. And that sent me a message about where their hearts— not just their words—really were. I have learned that whatever we undertake to teach, whether in a Sunday School setting or in our home, children learn at least as much by imitating us as by our deliberate instruction."

"Thanks, Kate." Alli recognizes the wisdom in Mother Earth's words. Indeed, children do imitate their parents. Then she turns her attention to Marilyn.

"I felt cheered on by my pastor when I was a high school student teaching the three year olds in Sunday School. He blessed me by showing he had confidence in me when he encouraged me to teach. Another person who greatly influenced my life and cheered me on was my sister. A musician, she was my mentor in music. When I was five, she began giving me piano lessons and accompanying me when I sang for various events. Not long ago I told her that she had had a great influence on my life; she was so surprised. I realized how neglectful we are of telling our own family members how much they mean to us."

Barbara reminisces. "God selects a variety of people to encourage us in His name. Life-shaping experiences are not limited to our growing-up years, but continue throughout our lives. A life-shaping experience occurred for me while at Concordia. Earlier I noted that I followed in my mother's footsteps, majoring in home economics. Ironically, my mother and I had the same teacher/advisor, Miss Krueger. When my mother died quite unexpectedly at age 43, her death impacted my life immensely. It was October of my junior year. During the several weeks I stayed home, I decided that I couldn't finish college. Being the oldest of three girls, with two sisters still in high school and no mother in the home, I felt responsible as a substitute mother. My dad and other relatives encouraged me to go back to school, reassuring me that my mother would have wanted me to graduate from Concordia. Financially it had been a hardship on my parents to send me to college, so that also entered into my quandary.

"Finally, I went to talk with my advisor, Miss Krueger. She convinced me to come back to school, to graduate with a degree in home economics, just like my mother. Although this advice may seem logical coming from a professor, it was very special to me. It was one-on-one counseling coming from someone who remembered my mother and who was concerned about me and my future. Miss Krueger is no longer living, but I am grateful that she cared enough to help me through this very rough time in my life and to show me the advantages of staying in college. Indeed, she helped shape my life. God used her to cheer me on."

Alli looks sad. "That's a touching story, Barbara. I don't think teachers realize how much influence they have on us. Elizabeth, your father also died when you were a teenager. Did that influence the rest of your life?"

"It is a painful experience for any teenager to lose a parent, but it didn't change my life that drastically. My mother and I continued living in our home. God influenced my mother and brother, since they chose Concordia for me, even though we weren't Lutheran. But they favored a church college close to home. I was willing to go, not knowing I'd end up with *this* bunch!"

Alli grins and notices Dana's gesture. "Singing in the college concert choir was certainly a life-shaping experience for me. God truly blessed me and cheered me on when He gave me an opportunity to sing in that wonderful choir. Our nationwide and European tours also added dimension to my college education. Praising our Lord through song is still the love of my life. Always will be!!"

"I'll be there to make your verses rhyme . . . "

"Earlier, I referred to nearly five hundred years of marriage in The Blue Garter Club," Alli says. "I don't want to belabor that point, but that is so noteworthy when so many of my classmates already have divorced, when broken homes are all too common, and many of today's households are headed by single parents." She emphasizes: "All of you say you asked Christ to be the key to your marriages and your homes, to create the One New Person relationships in which you have lived and grown. Most of you have seen the slogan: 'Families that pray together, stay together.' I do believe that. I guess you would all agree that God was there for you— to make your verses rhyme."

"I'll be there to guide you through the night . . . "

"Continuing with *Borning Cry*," Alli suggests with a teasing laugh, "perhaps that fourth verse depicts your present stage in life. The line *Not too old, no longer young* seems to fit you women!" Alli's facial expression changes. "Dana and Kate have given testimony to God's presence and sustaining strength of God when their husbands died. And in ways I'm only now coming to realize were so effective for me when my mother died. Others have thrown their lives into God's hands when their own health faced mortal threats. Barbara, you have faced cancer surgery, and you are certain that God led you through that dark night of fear to recovery and hope. Can you tell us about your ordeal?"

"I have had two onslaughts from cancer in the past twenty years," Barbara begins. "Although five years have elapsed since my last cancer bout, the word 'recovery' is still an elusive word to me. Yes, my fear is so real, but I do what I can regarding regular check-ups and tests. Then I ask Christ to take over.

"Some years ago, I started crabbing about my weight gain. My skirts no longer fit. I exercised a lot, to no avail. One night, I doubled over with excruciating pain in my stomach. Subsequent tests revealed an ovarian cyst. When results came back after surgery, the doctor told me it was malignant. He explained that as soon as I had regained some strength, I would have to undergo a complete hysterectomy. The doctor thought I was 28 years old instead of 38, so he hadn't performed a hysterectomy during the first surgery.

Alli looked at Barbara and again could understand the doctor's confusion about her age. Now she looks 38, not 58.

Barbara continues. "Many religious cards came during my hospital stay. I was sustained by Bible verses, particularly Philippians 4:13: *'I can do all things in him who strengthens me.'* [RSV] This verse encourages me to this day.

"Waiting between surgeries was difficult. Our children were young. I was needed at home. Although the children were helpful during this time, they were so afraid, and we didn't deal with those fears. Looking back, I realize our wish to protect them violated our children.

"Feeling completely helpless as I laid in a hospital bed during the second surgery, I once again turned my life over to God. Again I was sustained by a Bible verse and by God's promise. *'Have no anxiety about anything but in everything by prayer and supplication with thanksgiving let your requests be made known to God. And the peace of God, which passes all understanding, will keep your hearts and your minds in Christ Jesus.'* Philippians 4:6-7 [RSV]

"I didn't go through chemotherapy or radiation treatments because the doctors felt the surgery was successful. A couple of years later, I heard about the Cancer Detection Center in Minneapolis, so I began going there every other year for physicals with special emphasis on cancer detection. It was 15 years after my first cancer surgery when they found a tiny lump on my thyroid during one of these routine physicals. It was so small it could only be felt if I swallowed. A biopsy was done and when the results showed a malignancy, it was another crushing blow. Our daughter had had surgery the day of my biopsy, and while recovering, she and her husband stayed at our home. When the doctor called to tell me about the biopsy results, I was frying potatoes. After speaking to him, I returned to the stove in a stupor and scattered potatoes all over the place. Our son-in-law offered to finish the meal, suggesting I go off by myself to talk with Jesus. Again, our Lord was right there for me in this frightening moment.

"Before this latest surgery was performed, a friend shared with me a copy of the healing service with anointing of oil from our Lutheran *Book of Occasional Services*. This was the same healing service Kate arranged for Dan and others. When I told my pastor I wanted to have this healing service, he suggested it be a part of the regular Sunday service. It was a cleansing and truly blessed experience. The surgery went fine, but this time I also needed radioactive iodine treatments. I made regular visits to an oncologist.

"So many prayers were offered in my behalf, not only at our church, but at a Lutheran Church Women's Retreat. Lifted up before the throne of grace through a healing service and prayed for by friends and strangers alike, I was surrounded by such a sense of peace that I could accept whatever God had in store for me. Five years have gone by since that last surgery. I have hope, but having had two encounters, I am aware that I am in the high-risk cancer category.

"One thing I have noticed is that most people are reluctant to use the word 'cancer' when they inquire about my health. Cancer is a frightening ordeal, but talking about it helps, especially talking to someone who has been through similar surgery or treatment.

"Yes, God was there to guide me through the night— the dark night of cancer."

"Barbara, once again your life in Christ radiates to the rest of us." Alli notices tears being wiped away around this group. She thinks of her own mother who was taken away in the blink of an eye. Thank God she was such a strong Christian."

"I'll be there as I have always been . . . "

Turning to her notes, Alli redirects the conversation. "As life continues, several of you now find yourselves caring for elderly parents or other relatives. Sometimes called the 'sandwich' generation, women like you find that your energies at first go into raising your children. When that job is done, your attention turns to helping aging parents. If you are also working at a full-time job, there's little energy left for marriage and parenting. Who wants to talk about your 'sandwich' generation experience? Dana?"

"Yes, I did care for my aging parents, who lived next door to us for several years until their deaths. Being an only child can be difficult because you have no help in decision making. My husband had heart surgery; my mother had a major stroke and was hospitalized in July and died in August; my dad had to go into a nursing home because his Alzheimer-like condition made it impossible for him to live alone. My whole family was collapsing—all at once.

"God was there as He always had been when the evening gently closed in for my parents. Not only did He give them strength in their last days, but He kept me going to care for these dearest people who needed me. I could not have carried on alone.

"My experience with the 'sandwich' generation fits your description very well," concludes Dana.

Alli looks at Barbara and says, "You have also expressed concern about the aged. What's your experience as part of the 'sandwich' generation?"

"My father has been a widower for nearly forty years. Raising my two younger sisters alone after our mother died, he is a wonderful example of a Christian father. Since his heart attack, Dad doesn't have his former zip. It hurts us to see him inactive when we remember how he was always running and playing ball with his grandchildren; now he sits and watches. When I ask him how he feels, he says he feels 85! Yes, his evening is gently closing in, but God has sustained my father through these many years and made him such a blessing to all who know him.

"We have also cared for John's aunt. A widow without a family, she was like a grandmother to our children. During my cancer surgeries, she helped care for our children. When her personality began changing a few years ago, we were alarmed. She is now doing quite well on medication for depression."

Sally speaks up, "Is this the person you took to the doctor for testing, Barbara?"

With a wan smile, Barbara answers, "Yes. There are memory tests used to help diagnose Alzheimers. The doctor would tell Aunt Ida three places or three things to remember; then later he asked her to recall them. Listening to this testing procedure, I was the one who could not remember the third place or thing! Aunt Ida did fine! It almost put me into a panic!"

Smiling, Alli looks at both Elizabeth and Renae, commenting that each of them is in the 'sandwich' generation. Elizabeth speaks first: "My mother is 87, lives alone, and is still somewhat independent. Having a parent in this age bracket produces some anxiety because there are numerous things that could happen—such as a fall. But one of my greatest concerns is that she still drives her car. Older people don't like to give up their independence, and since my mother has been a widow for over forty years, her car is one important symbol of independence to her. Fortunately she doesn't drive very much or very far.

"Over the years, she has lived with us off and on, so our children know their grandmother well—for which I am thankful. The evening is gently closing in, and she has maintained her faith through these many years. God was there for her."

Renae describes her role in the 'sandwich' generation. "My mother is 83, lives alone in an apartment
about five minutes from us. She manages well and
needs very little help. In fact, over the years she has been
a tremendous help to us in caring for Travis. She still is
a truly special, wonderful person whom we all enjoy.
She's still growing in Christ, and she is still growing as
a person. So, her age hasn't made much difference, so
far."

"Laura?"

"My mother is 92 and as sharp as ever. She lives in a
retirement home in Wisconsin. A religious up-bringing
and my college education are treasured gifts from my
parents; these can never be taken away. Most of us here
were raised by Christian parents; our children and grandchildren will be the beneficiaries.

"As the words of the hymn confirm, *'I'll be there as I
have always been,'* generation after generation will know
the same God. I remember the times Jack's mother
visited us in Pittsburgh. Those were days when I first
experienced the Biblical meaning of passing the Birthright. Our young children would lead her to the porch
swing where they would cluster around her and beg,
"Now, tell us the stories, Grandma. She was getting
senile, but her memory for distant past was still vivid. I
recall how Jack would sidle over to them to eavesdrop
on her tales of family generations long ago—tales he'd
never heard before. Aged parents may not function well
in other ways, but they can do so well in passing the
Birthright, if we will invest them with that vocation.
They should be the living bridges of Alpha-Omega for
our families, from past generations through future ones,
right now."

Alli responds. "Let me tell you that each one of you in
this room is passing me the Birthright as you tell the
stories that included my mother and explained the times

in which she matured. I shall go back to my Grandmother to learn more about Mom in her pre-college days. Thank you, thank you!"

The women all nod, and Celia adds. "Maybe the term 'sandwich generation' has more than one meaning. We have spoken of caring for elderly parents after our own children are grown. Another aspect of the sandwich generation might be one of how we bridge the generational gap between our parents' traditional ways and our children's modern ways. We may be pulled in both directions. Some traditions we don't want to lose, such as commitment to marriage, family and the church. Other traditions such as how a woman is addressed— Mrs. or Ms.—aren't terribly important to us. Some of our daughters have kept their maiden names after marriage or used hyphenated versions."

Alli adds, "The bridging Celia spoke of can go another direction, too. Sometimes grandparents become a bridge between parents and children. That has happened often in my home. Now, you women have become a bridge between me and who my mother was."

Sally comments, "Bridges—yes, that's a good point, Alli. I want to add that while our own mothers seldom worked outside the home, our generation usually had a choice of being a full-time homemaker or combining homemaking with work outside the home. But our children's generation, for the most part, has little choice in today's economy: both husband and wife *must* work for pay."

Dana continues. "Our 'sandwich generation' is often caught in the middle trying to hang on to the vital heritage of our parents' generation, and also trying to understand the musical TV videos our children listen to. Our family talks about the dilemma this puts us in. But, once again, we keep getting our bearings from our Lord God, who is there now as He has always been."

"I've noticed how much more our children come right out with 'I love you,'" Marilyn notes. "This is certainly contrary to our up-bringing when parents rarely verbalized their love or praise. We knew our parents loved us, but they seemed embarrassed to express it. Our generation has probably learned from our children how to express love more openly."

From across the room we hear, "I agree. One of the most hurtful experiences of my life was saying good-bye to my father just before he died. He could not tell me he loved me. Our children will not have that experience because our generation has learned the value of love openly expressed. Few of us learned that by our parents' example."

"And we want to make sure that this love is unconditional, like God's love," adds Sarah. "Parents we've known are often guilty of giving 'dog love,' meaning that if a child performs, he'll get a pat on the back. But those parents forget to love the child just for being a part of the family."

Claudia speaks up on another concern. "Our generation was born during the Depression and raised by parents who knew what it meant to 'go without.' We learned to conserve. Our children, on the other hand, can be very wasteful. This is another one of those generation gaps, but one where we need to emphasize the importance of our heritage. What our Depression childhood knew, today's generation confronts as conserving the environment. Not as a God in itself, I hope, but as the world God so loved."

"Reduce, Reuse, Recycle has to be our motto," chants Celia. "Recycling isn't new. It's what all of us grew up with in childhood. Remember rolling into a ball the silver wrappers for the war effort? Mom altered my dresses to fit my younger sisters, and she sat in the rocking chair darning Dad's sox. Then, of course, the Blue Garter Club recycled a certain blue garter."

Laura adds, "Our daughter wore my sister's wedding dress that my mother sewed for her in 1952. With the up-dated neckline, its gorgeous fabric couldn't be bought today. So we did some heartfelt recycling!"

"Thanks to all of you for opening your lives to me, as you have done with each other through the years with your Round Robin," says Alli, looking again at her notes for the final portion of this chapter. Audrey raises her hand.

"When we talk about the evening gently closing in, I am reminded of God's promise to provide us with our eternal home. Watching beautiful sunsets over the lake near our home, we often comment that heaven must be like that. Last month we attended the funeral of a loved one and were comforted by the words of John 14:1-3:

> 'Let not your hearts be troubled; believe in God, believe also in me. In my Father's house are many rooms; if it were not so would I have told you that I go to prepare a place for you? And when I go and prepare a place for you, I will come again and will take you to myself that where I am you may be also.'" [RSV]

*"I was there to hear your borning cry . . .
To see your life unfold."*

"How did your life unfold? What does it mean to live happily ever after?" Alli asks as the last session draws to a close. "Judging from what you have shared here, Blue Garter Club members know what living happily ever after does **not** mean. It does **not** mean a life free of hardships, pain and suffering. It does **not** mean that either you or your spouse has found the perfect mate. It does **not** mean that you know how to raise model children. And, it does **not** mean that your vocation will do wonders financially.

"But, it *does* mean that in spite of being surrounded by imperfect people, in spite of hardships and setbacks, your life has real meaning. You can look back on a life punctured with grief and heartache and still say, 'I have had a good life. Yes, I did live happily ever after. God didn't promise me a rose garden, but God promised to be with me through every thorny or fragrant episode. God was there to see my life unfold.'"

Continuing, Alli looks at a typewritten paper, then back at the group. "I want to share some final thoughts on heritage, on tradition, on ties that bind. You have emphasized the rich Christian heritage of your birth, the traditional values you have placed on raising your own children in that Christian faith, and the Christian ties that bind all of you in The Blue Garter Club.

"Laura brought all of these ideas together, when expressing her thoughts after the Baccalaureate service as their youngest child graduated from college."

"Hallelujah! Our last child has completed college. No more tuition payments! That was my very irreverent thought as we headed off to Texas Lutheran College for our son's Baccalaureate service. It never dawned on me that this might just happen to be a moving experience and that I might even feel a wave of sadness or melancholy. As we entered that steepled chapel, the pipe organ sounds soared like a mighty wind. There stood our son behind the altar, ready to lead the liturgy. It was Mother's Day, 1992.

*"'The Ties That Bind' was the Baccalaureate theme, and, of course, we sang **Blest Be the Ties That Bind**. Not only did I think of our Blue Garter Club members, but I contemplated the thousands of times this hymn has been sung in Christian churches throughout the world. Singing this familiar hymn while the sun shone through the stained-glass windows brought the words 'tradition' and 'heritage' to my mind.*

"After the homily, we sang John Ylvisaker's hymn, **I Was There To Hear Your Borning Cry**. Singing this hymn always turns me into a sniveling fool. The woman next to me was dabbing at her eyes and that was reassuring to me. Once again I thought of 'heritage' and 'tradition,' because my mind wandered back to Concordia's Centennial Homecoming, when thousands of us joined in singing that same hymn at the campus worship service on Sunday, October 13, 1991. At that service, Sue, our daughter, and I had exchanged nervous glances, knowing both of us become unglued while singing that song.

"My thoughts returned to the present service. As I attempted to regain my composure, our son stood up to speak the liturgy on family ties. Enough already!! Bring me a crying towel! Heritage. Tradition.

"Then the Texas Lutheran Choir was ready to perform. Paul J. Christiansen's son, 'Coach,' as his adoring choir members call him, directed his grandfather's classic arrangement of **Beautiful Savior**. My sister sang it in the Concordia Concert Choir in 1950. Now our son was singing it in a concert choir in 1992. Heritage. Tradition.

"A feeling of gratitude and awe swept through me. Gratitude that we are a part of this rich tradition and heritage of our family's religious faith and commitment. I felt rich, despite all those tuition payments! This richness certainly transcends dollar signs and debts. The wealth of tradition is carried on through our children and their children, from generation to generation.

Thanks be to God—our Alpha and Omega!"

And now it is time to say . . .

Farewell

After almost three days of intensive chattering, sharing, and reminiscing, the Blue Garter Club members gather their belongings and load their cars. They know it will be several years before they get together again like this. Before they say their final farewells, Claudia asks that they come into the den.

Alli looks at fourteen Blue Garter Members and says, "You have been a bridge from my past to my present. You have given me my Birthright; you have told me the stories about my mother's era that had been a mystery to me. You've taught me about God-given strength in the face of tragedy and family trials. You've impressed on me the values of heritage and tradition. I am eternally grateful. Thank you, my mother's friends, and mine."

"Alli, thank you for coming to our reunion. It was a supreme pleasure to have you with us. This group may have a hundred different opinions on almost everything, but we all agreed on two things last evening after you had retired to your room. We wish to pass to you our venerable Blue Garter, and we hope you will do us the great honor of accepting our invitation to be the next generation's charter member of The Blue Garter Club."

. . . And then there were fifteen, once more!

I WAS THERE TO HEAR YOUR BORNING CRY

John Ylvisaker

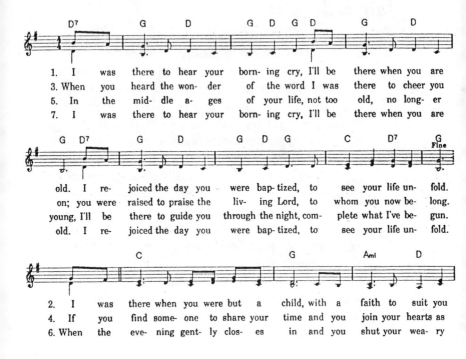

1. I was there to hear your born- ing cry, I'll be there when you are
3. When you heard the won- der of the word I was there to cheer you
5. In the mid- dle a- ges of your life, not too old, no long- er
7. I was there to hear your born- ing cry, I'll be there when you are

old. I re- joiced the day you were bap- tized, to see your life un- fold.
on; you were raised to praise the liv- ing Lord, to whom you now be- long.
young, I'll be there to guide you through the night, com- plete what I've be- gun.
old. I re- joiced the day you were bap- tized, to see your life un- fold.

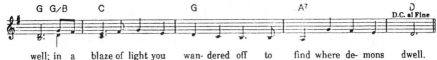

2. I was there when you were but a child, with a faith to suit you
4. If you find some- one to share your time and you join your hearts as
6. When the eve- ning gent- ly clos- es in and you shut your wea- ry

well; in a blaze of light you wan- dered off to find where de- mons dwell.
one, I'll be there to make your vers- es rhyme from dusk 'til ris- ing sun.
eyes, I'll be there as I have al- ways been with just one more sur- prise.

Index of Poetry

Bibliography

Lewis, C.S., *MERE CHRISTIANITY*, Collier Books, MacMillan Publishing Company, 1952 edition, p. 95.

Lewis, Daphne, *ILLUMINATIONS: An Interweave of Thought, Identity, and Love*, LangMarc Publishing, © 1992, "Whose Fault," p. 86; "His Mama's Gift," p. 92.

Qualben, Lois, *SAND CASTLES AND FORTRESSES*, LangMarc Publishing, © 1991, "Loneliness," p. 49; "Time is Short," p. 123.

Scripture taken from the *HOLY BIBLE, Revised Standard Version*, New Testament Section, © 1946; Old Testament Section, © 1952.

Ylvisaker, John, "I Was There To Hear Your Borning Cry," Permission granted from New Generation Publishers, Box 321, Waverly, IA 50677.

To Order Copies

☎ **Telephone Orders:** Call 1-800-864-1648

✉ **Postal Orders:** LangMarc Publishing, P.O. Box 33817, San Antonio, Texas 78265-3817. USA.

The Blue Garter Club

Number of soft cover copies _____ x $11.95 = $ _____

Quantity Discounts: 10% discount for 3-4 copies, 15% discount for 5-9 copies, 20% discount for 10 or more copies.

Shipping: Unless requested otherwise, sent UPS.
   UPS: $2.50 for first book and 75¢ for each additional book. (Delivery usually five week days)
   Book Rate: $1.50 for the first book and 50¢ for each additional book. (Delivery up to three weeks)

Sales Tax: Texas residents please add 7.25% (87¢ for 1 book)

Send a Friend a Gift: We will gift wrap, enclose gift card and mail directly. Shipping cost to each address will be $2.50 UPS or $1.50 Book Rate.

Please send payment with order.

Books Cost: _____

Shipping: _____

Check Enclosed: _____

Name and UPS Address for order delivery:

_____

_____

_____

_____